ECONOMIC CONDITIONS IN FOREIGN COUNTRIES

1932–1933

ECONOMIC CONDITIONS
IN FOREIGN COUNTRIES
1932–1933

NATIONAL INDUSTRIAL CONFERENCE BOARD, Inc.
NEW YORK
1933

May, 1933
197

FOREWORD

O N THE eve of the International Economic Conference there seems to be a growing confidence throughout the world that the low point of the business depression has been reached and left behind, and that in the absence of unfavorable developments in the political field the beginning of a revival in industrial and trade activity is to be expected in the second half of 1933. The constructive accomplishments that are in a large measure responsible for this feeling of optimism may be listed as follows:

1. The conclusion of the Lausanne agreement, removing the question of reparations from the field of politics.

2. The balancing of the British budget and political stabilization in Great Britain, which restored confidence in the British financial and economic system.

3. The successful conversions of internal debts of the governments of Great Britain and France.

4. The marked stability of the prices of world staple commodities since the summer of 1932.

5. The dramatic reversal of the disastrous process of deflation in the United States in the spring of 1933.

6. The initiative taken by the President of the United States in breaking the international deadlock by inviting the heads of foreign governments to Washington for personal discussion of world economic and political problems.

7. The decision made after the Washington conversations to convene the International Economic Conference in London on June 12, 1933.

8. The acceptance by the leading nations of the world of the American proposal for a tariff truce until the International Economic Conference finishes its work.

The importance of these constructive accomplishments, however, must not be overestimated. The difficulties that lie ahead are extremely grave. World trade is strangled by innumerable restrictions on the international movement of goods, in the form of excessive tariffs, import quotas, licensing systems, foreign exchange controls, clearing agreements,

v

and so on. World currencies are unstable, and in most countries the value of the exchanges as stated in the official quotations is purely nominal, owing to prohibition of free dealings in foreign exchange. An enormous volume of short-term foreign credits is frozen, while an even larger volume of long-term foreign debts is in default. In addition, the financial position of many governments remains extremely precarious.

The political relations among some of the leading countries are in a state of extreme tension, while open warfare, although without a declaration of war, is carried on in the Far East. Furthermore, the internal political conditions in many countries are ominous, and the threat of revolutions and internal disorders endangers economic revival and world peace.

The Continent of Europe is in turmoil. The cause of the conflict is the Treaty of Versailles. In the course of the last decade the movement for a peaceful revision of the Treaty has gained numerous adherents, and the justice of many claims put forward by the advocates of revision is not denied by neutral observers at the present time. Recent developments at the Disarmament Conference and the statements issued by the Governments of the United States, Great Britain, France, and Germany indicate that treaty revision by means of another war will not be tolerated by the leading countries of the world. Most of the wars in modern history have been fought to bring about revision of treaties that to some countries appeared inequitable, and all wars have resulted in the conclusion of treaties that some countries regarded as intolerable. If the extraordinary developments in the field of international politics that have taken place in recent weeks are to be interpreted as a sign that the principal countries of the world have come to realize that international difficulties can never be adjusted by means of war and that war always creates new difficulties, a great advance has been made toward the maintenance of peace and the orderly progress of civilized society.

In his message to the sovereigns and presidents of fifty-four nations, sent on May 16, 1933, the President of the United States stated that the "ultimate objective of the disarmament conference must be the complete elimination of all offensive weapons" and that in the present discussions the nations should agree: "First, to take, at once, the first definite step toward this objective, as broadly outlined in the MacDonald plan. Second, to agree upon a time and procedure for taking the following steps. Third, to agree that while the first and the following steps are being taken, no nation shall increase its existing armaments over and above the limitations of treaty obligations." The President, however, went further than this and proposed that "all nations of the world should enter into a solemn and definite pact of non-aggression; that they should solemnly reaffirm the obligations they have assumed to limit and reduce their armaments, and, provided these obligations are faithfully executed by all signatory powers, individually agree that they will send no armed force of whatsoever nature across their frontiers."[1]

The MacDonald Disarmament Plan, mentioned by the President, was presented to the Disarmament Conference on March 16, 1933. Part I of the Plan deals with the question of security; Part II, with disarmament provisions; Part III, with the exchange of information; Part IV, with the prohibition of chemical warfare; and Part V, with general provisions, Permanent Disarmament Commission, exceptions, etc. Under this plan the land forces of Continental Europe would be put on a comparable basis. In order to limit the power of aggression they would be reduced to a militia basis by fixing 8 months as the maximum period of service, with the provision that the length of service could be extended to 12 months in certain cases to be decided by the Conference. The military strength of the principal European powers, as thus limited, would be as follows:

Country	Home Forces	Overseas Forces
France	200,000	200,000
Germany	200,000	..
Italy	200,000	50,000
Poland	200,000	..
Czechoslovakia	100,000	..
Jugoslavia	100,000	..
Hungary	60,000	..
Austria	50,000	..

[1] "The New York Times," New York, May 17, 1933, p. 1.

The acceptance of the MacDonald Plan by Chancellor Hitler in his address of May 17, 1933, following the strong backing that it has received from Great Britain, the United States, France, and Italy, may have saved the World Disarmament Conference from collapse and increased the chances for success of the International Economic Conference. There appears to be a universal recognition of the fact that another great war would mean a collapse of the present civilization. So far as the international political factors are concerned, the immediate outlook for world economic recovery is, therefore, better than it has been at any time since the beginning of the business depression.

Following the policy established in 1928, the Conference Board presents in this book a brief review of the outstanding developments in world economy and economic conditions in individual foreign countries in the preceding year and in the early part of 1933. The special articles of the Foreign Correspondents of the Conference Board have been omitted from this volume and are being published in a series of independent monographs.[1] The Board wishes to take this opportunity again to thank its Foreign Correspondents for their generous co-operation and assistance in the collection and interpretation of factual information not only concerning the economic situation in their individual countries but also in regard to affairs of general international importance.

The investigation on which this publication is based was made by Mr. Vaso Trivanovitch, of the Conference Board's Research Staff, and the text was prepared by him under the supervision of the Staff Economic Council.

VIRGIL JORDAN
President

New York City
May, 1933

---

[1] The following articles have been published already: Sir Lennon Raws, "Possibilities of Economic Recovery in Australia"; Mr. Li Ming and S. Ikeda, "Economic Aspects of Sino-Japanese Relations"; Sir Arthur Balfour, "War Debts: The British Viewpoint"; Mr. R. P. Duchemin, "The Tariff Policy of France"; Mr. A. S. Benni, "Business Reorganization in Italy." Special monographs concerning the situation in the Netherlands, Switzerland, Belgium, Denmark, Austria, Jugoslavia, Hungary, and Argentina will be issued shortly.

CONTENTS

LIST OF TABLES

ECONOMIC CONDITIONS IN FOREIGN COUNTRIES

I

GENERAL SURVEY

INTERNATIONAL TRADE

THE total value of foreign trade of 25 countries, which account for more than 80% of total world trade, declined from $31,483 million in 1931 to $20,756 million in 1932, as shown in Table 1. The value of foreign trade of these countries was $43,913 million in 1930 and $55,340 million in 1929. The decline from 1929 to 1932 amounted to $34,584 million, or 62%. From 1931 to 1932 the decline was 34%.

The countries shown in the table are divided into creditor and debtor countries. The creditor countries are those whose income from foreign investments is larger than the payment that they have to make to foreign holders of their own securities. Debtor countries are those that pay more to foreign investors than they receive from their investments abroad.

A debtor country can make payments on account of foreign investments by means of a surplus of commodity and service exports, or by borrowing abroad, or by shipping gold. In each year from 1924 to 1930, with the exception of 1926, the debtor countries as a whole had a surplus of commodity imports. During the same period most of the debtor countries had deficits in their balance of payments on account of shipping services and insurance and banking commissions. Tourist expenditures and emigrant remittances were important items in the case of some of the debtor countries, but were of little importance to a large majority of the debtor nations. The debtor countries were able to pay for their surplus of commodity imports largely by means of additional

1

TABLE 1: VALUE OF EXPORTS AND IMPORTS, 25 COUNTRIES, 1924 TO 1932

Source: League of Nations; United States Department of Commerce

In million dollars

Country	1924	1925	1926	1927	1928	1929	1930	1931	1932	Percentage Decline 1929 to 1932	Percentage Decline 1931 to 1932
Creditor Countries											
United States											
Exports	4,591	4,910	4,809	4,865	5,128	5,241	3,843	2,424	1,612	69.2	33.5
Imports	3,610	4,227	4,431	4,185	4,091	4,399	3,061	2,091	1,323	69.9	36.7
Great Britain											
Exports	4,156	4,478	3,782	4,049	4,106	4,083	3,200	2,061	1,459	64.3	29.2
Imports	5,643	6,378	6,031	5,929	5,825	5,941	5,081	3,906	2,465	58.5	36.9
France											
Exports	2,219	2,222	1,920	2,153	2,013	1,966	1,679	1,193	772	60.7	35.3
Imports	2,103	2,125	1,932	2,080	2,095	2,282	2,058	1,654	1,169	48.8	29.3
Netherlands											
Exports	635	726	701	762	798	800	691	527	340	57.5	35.5
Imports	903	986	979	1,022	1,079	1,106	972	761	522	52.8	31.4
Belgium											
Exports	641	702	650	740	859	883	725	643	412	53.3	35.9
Imports	821	850	751	808	889	985	860	660	452	54.1	31.5
Switzerland											
Exports	364	392	353	386	408	401	337	258	148	63.1	42.6
Imports	453	481	456	483	512	516	488	428	330	36.0	22.9
Sweden											
Exports	334	365	380	432	422	486	416	283	174	64.2	38.5
Imports	378	388	399	425	458	478	446	357	212	55.6	40.6
Total exports	12,940	13,795	12,595	13,388	13,734	13,860	10,891	7,389	4,917	64.5	33.5
Total imports	13,911	15,435	14,979	14,932	14,949	15,707	12,966	9,857	6,473	58.8	34.3

Debtor Countries

Germany											
Exports	1,561	2,213	2,481	2,573	2,924	3,212	2,867	2,286	1,367	57.4	40.2
Imports	2,164	2,945	2,382	3,389	3,335	3,203	2,476	1,602	1,114	65.2	30.5
Italy											
Exports	627	727	726	806	764	801	638	523	358	55.3	31.5
Imports	845	1,043	1,007	1,051	1,159	1,140	912	606	435	61.8	28.2
Czechoslovakia											
Exports	503	557	529	596	628	607	517	389	217	64.3	44.2
Imports	468	522	452	532	568	592	465	349	221	62.7	36.7
Denmark											
Exports	360	414	398	415	443	459	433	335	213	53.6	36.4
Imports	396	440	425	444	465	481	463	368	215	55.3	41.6
Norway											
Exports	149	188	181	178	183	202	183	116	102	49.5	12.1
Imports	214	247	244	254	271	288	285	215	124	56.9	42.3
Austria											
Exports	277	266	240	286	310	308	261	184	106	65.6	42.4
Imports	485	397	389	434	447	459	380	304	194	57.7	36.2
Hungary											
Exports	117	142	152	140	143	182	159	99	58	68.1	41.4
Imports	142	150	166	200	208	186	144	96	59	68.3	38.5
Poland											
Exports	244	248	252	282	281	316	273	211	122	61.4	42.2
Imports	285	295	173	325	377	349	252	164	97	72.2	40.9
Jugoslavia											
Exports	122	152	138	113	113	139	120	85	50	64.0	41.2
Imports	105	149	135	128	138	134	123	85	47	64.9	44.7
Canada											
Exports	1,057	1,283	1,284	1,239	1,374	1,208	906	595	435	64.0	26.9
Imports	798	890	1,008	1,087	1,222	1,299	1,009	611	399	69.3	34.7
Argentina											
Exports	790	793	730	972	987	907	513	428	331	63.5	22.7
Imports	648	801	758	825	875	820	617	345	215	73.8	37.7
Brazil											
Exports	423	491	461	432	475	456	311	239	182	60.1	23.8
Imports	305	412	391	388	442	417	251	131	105	74.8	19.8

3

TABLE 1: VALUE OF EXPORTS AND IMPORTS, 25 COUNTRIES, 1924 TO 1932—(Continued)

Source: League of Nations; United States Department of Commerce

In million dollars

Country	1924	1925	1926	1927	1928	1929	1930	1931	1932	Percentage Decline 1929 to 1932	Percentage Decline 1931 to 1932
Chile											
Exports	201	227	201	211	239	277	160	112	28	89.9	75.0
Imports	120	148	156	130	142	195	169	86	17	91.3	80.2
Colombia											
Exports	86	83	110	106	114	123	109	95	67	45.5	29.5
Imports	55	87	109	123	123	122	61	40	29	76.2	27.5
India											
Exports	1,216	1,476	1,196	1,186	1,234	1,191	927	573	357	70.0	37.7
Imports	775	820	849	896	906	900	667	464	350	61.1	24.6
Australia											
Exports	628	763	710	714	674	600	424	322	268	55.3	16.8
Imports	642	769	772	787	681	707	460	197	186	73.7	5.6
Japan											
Exports	744	946	964	945	915	991	726	566	383	61.4	32.3
Imports	1,011	1,056	1,120	1,033	1,019	1,022	764	610	390	61.8	36.1
China											
Exports	642	667	672	648	714	660	420	314	168	74.5	46.5
Imports	842	811	870	714	859	820	611	492	357	56.5	27.4
Total Exports	9,747	11,636	11,425	11,842	12,515	12,639	9,947	7,472	4,812	61.9	35.6
Total Imports	10,300	11,982	11,406	12,740	13,237	13,134	10,109	6,765	4,554	65.3	32.7
Grand Total Exports	22,687	25,431	24,020	25,230	26,249	26,499	20,838	14,861	9,729	63.3	34.5
Imports	24,211	27,417	26,385	27,672	28,186	28,841	23,075	16,622	11,027	61.8	33.7

foreign borrowing. This, however, came to an end in 1930, when the export of capital from Great Britain and the United States ceased.

The effect of this development is shown in the trade figures for 1931. From 1930 to 1931 the value of exports of the debtor countries declined from $9,947 million to $7,472 million, while the value of imports declined from $10,109 million to $6,765 million. In 1930 the debtor countries had a surplus of commodity imports of $162 million. In 1931 this import surplus was changed into a surplus of commodity exports of $707 million. From 1930 to 1931 the four leading South American countries—Argentina, Brazil, Chile, and Colombia—reduced the value of their imports by 45.2%, while the value of their exports declined only 20.0%. During the same period German imports declined 35.3%, while the reduction in German exports was only 20.3%. The corresponding figures for Poland are 34.9% and 22.7%; for Italy, 33.6% and 18.0%, and for Australia, 57.2% and 24.1%. While these adjustments were being made in the balance of payments of the debtor countries, the movement of trade in the creditor countries was in the opposite direction, that is, the decline of exports was greater than that of imports.

This process of adjustment, however, came to an end in 1932. In 1931, the debtor countries were able to reduce their imports by drastic restrictions that were introduced against foreign products by means of quotas, licenses, control of foreign exchange transactions, and similar impediments to trade. In 1932, similar prohibitions were introduced by the creditor countries. From 1931 to 1932, the decline in the value of exports of the debtor countries was 35.6%, as compared with a decline in imports of 32.7%, while the value of exports of the creditor countries declined 33.5%, and that of imports, 34.3%. In most of the debtor countries the decline in exports from 1929 to 1932 was considerably larger than the decline in imports, while the contrary is true of the creditor countries.

International Movement of Gold

The years 1931 and 1932 were characterized by extraordinary movements of gold. The nature of the flow of gold in

1932, however, was different from that in 1931. The enormous depletion of the gold reserves of the debtor countries that took place in 1931 came to an end in the course of 1932. The gold reserves of the central banks and governments of the 7 creditor countries, shown in Table 2, increased from $8,557 million at the end of 1931 to $9,190 million at the end of 1932, or $633 million. Of this increase, France alone accounted for $555 million. The gold reserves of the 33 debtor countries during the same period declined by $105 million. In 1931 the gold reserves of the creditor countries were increased by $949 million, and those of the debtor countries were reduced by $688 million. The loss of gold by the debtor countries in 1932 was due almost entirely to the decline in the gold holdings of Germany and Japan. Most of the debtor countries were able to prevent further depletion of their gold reserves in 1932, and in a number of these countries the holdings of gold actually increased.

The total world production of gold in 1932 is estimated at about $500 million, showing an increase of approximately $40 million, as compared with 1931. In addition to the output of new gold from the mines, the monetary stock of gold was increased in 1932 by about $220 million through the release of gold from the private holdings in India. The output of newly mined gold and the total addition to the world's supply of gold were the highest on record in 1932.

At the end of 1932 the United States held 35.4% of the total gold reserves, as compared with 37.1% at the end of 1931. France was able in 1932 to increase her share of the gold supply from 24.7% to 28.4%. The 7 creditor countries combined held 80.3% of the total gold reserves at the end of 1932, as compared with 78.4% a year ago, while the proportion held by the 33 debtor countries declined from 21.6% to 19.7%.

The gold holdings of the Bank of France reached their peak on December 8, 1932, when they amounted to 83,359 million francs, $3,268 million. By March 23, 1933, the French gold reserve was reduced to 80,788 million francs, $3,167 million, a loss of approximately $100 million. The gold reserve of the Bank of England reached the low point of £120.5 million, $586 million, on January 12, 1933. Since that time the Bank of England has been able steadily to increase its gold holdings until they amounted to £170.4 million, $829 million, on March 23, 1933.

TABLE 2: GOLD RESERVES OF CENTRAL BANKS AND GOVERN-MENTS OF 40 COUNTRIES, END OF 1913 AND 1924 TO 1932

In million dollars

Country	1913	1924	1925	1926	1927	1928	1929	1930	1931	1932
Creditor Countries										
United States	1,290	4,090	3,985	4,083	3,977	3,746	3,900	4,225	4,051	4,045
Great Britain	165	748	695	729	737	748	710	718	588	583
France	679	710	711	711	954	1,254	1,633	2,100	2,699	3,254
Belgium	48	53	53	86	100	126	163	191	354	361
Switzerland	33	98	90	91	100	103	115	136	453	477
Netherlands	61	203	178	166	161	175	180	171	357	415
Sweden	27	64	62	60	62	63	66	65	55	55
Total	2,303	5,966	5,774	5,926	6,091	6,215	6,767	7,608	8,557	9,190
Debtor Countries										
Europe										
Germany	279	181	288	436	444	650	544	528	234	192
Italy	267	221	222	224	242	266	273	279	296	307
Austria	..	2	2	7	12	24	24	30	27	21
Poland	..	20	26	27	58	70	79	63	67	56
Rumania	29	48	49	50	51	49	55	56	58	57
Jugoslavia	11	14	15	17	17	18	18	19	31	31
Hungary	..	7	10	30	34	35	28	28	18	17
Bulgaria	11	8	8	8	9	10	10	10	11	11
Denmark	20	56	56	56	49	46	46	46	39	36
Czechoslovakia	..	27	27	27	30	34	37	46	49	51
Estonia	..	1	1	1	1	2	2	2	2	2
Finland	7	8	8	8	8	8	8	8	8	2
Latvia	..	5	5	5	5	5	5	5	6	2
Lithuania	..	3	3	3	3	3	4	4	5	2
Greece	5	12	13	14	15	7	8	7	11	8
Norway	12	39	39	39	39	39	39	39	41	39
Portugal	8	9	9	9	9	9	9	9	13	23
Spain	92	489	489	493	502	494	495	470	434	436
America										
Canada	117	151	157	158	152	114	78	110	78	84
Argentina	256	444	451	451	529	607	434	412	253	249
Brazil	90	54	54	56	101	149	150	11	2	2
Chile	1[1]	34	34	10	7	7	8	7	12	10
Colombia	..	9	15	18	20	24	22	17	9	12
Peru	2[1]	22	22	22	24	22	22	18	17	11
Mexico	..	..	17	5	6	6	7	4	2	2
Uruguay	11	57	57	57	59	68	68	60	53	48
Asia										
India	124	109	109	109	119	124	128	128	162	162
Japan	65	586	576	562	542	541	542	412	234	212
Java	10	54	73	79	72	68	56	56	45	42
Australia	22	130	162	110	106	109	90	75	52	42
New Zealand	25	38	38	38	38	35	32	33	32	27
Africa										
Egypt	10	17	17	17	18	18	19	20	21	33
South Africa	34	53	44	37	40	39	36	33	39	35
Total	1,508	2,908	3,096	3,183	3,361	3,700	3,376	3,045	2,357	2,252
Grand Total	3,811	8,874	8,870	9,109	9,452	9,915	10,143	10,653	10,914	11,442

[1] 1914.
[2] Not available.

3

The gold reserves of the debtor countries were consider ably lower at the end of 1932 than in any year since the close of the World War. From 1920 to 1924, which was a period of world-wide currency dislocation, the gold reserves of the debtor countries remained practically unchanged. During the 5-year period, 1925 to 1929, the debtor countries increased their gold holdings by $468 million. This was a period of extensive foreign loans from the United States and Great Britain. During this period the gold standard was restored in practically every country of the world.[1]

The sudden cessation of long-term international financing in 1930 and the extraordinary flight of short-term capital from the debtor countries to the creditor countries undermined the entire financial structure of the world in 1931 and led to formal abandonment of the gold standard in 27 countries and to the introduction of some form of foreign exchange control in all countries with the exception of France, Switzerland, the Netherlands, and Belgium. In addition, 17 debtor countries proclaimed complete or partial moratoria on foreign debt service.

The world today is faced with an enormous task of financial reconstruction. Revival of international trade cannot take place so long as foreign exchange control, import quotas, and other quantitative restrictions on imports are practised by most countries of the world. So far, however, as these restrictions have been adopted by the debtor nations to protect whatever gold reserve they have left and to create or maintain a surplus of commodity exports, their removal cannot be expected until the creditor countries agree on some plan of action to raise world community prices and thus decrease the enormous burden of indebtedness incurred by the debtor countries from 1924 to 1930.

COMMODITY PRICES

About the middle of 1932 there occurred a slight improvement in world prices of raw materials and foodstuffs, which affected a large number of world staple commodities—coffee, wheat, sugar, cotton, rubber, silk, wool, hides and leather.

[1] China, Brazil, Honduras, Persia, Spain, Turkey, and Uruguay are the only countries that did not adopt the gold standard after the World War.

TABLE 3: INDEX NUMBERS OF WORLD PRICES OF RAW MATERIALS AND FOODSTUFFS, 1929 TO 1933

Base, 1923–25 = 100

Source: U. S. Department of Commerce

Year and Month	Wheat[1]	Sugar[2]	Coffee[3]	Cotton[4]	Rubber[5]	Silk[6]	Copper[7]	Tin[8]
1929, January	83.3	50.6	118.6	74.3	47.2	69.8	120.0	97.8
February	85.8	48.9	121.6	74.3	56.1	71.2	128.2	98.2
March	83.3	48.4	122.6	77.9	57.5	69.8	153.7	97.2
April	79.5	46.6	121.1	73.9	49.6	71.9	141.0	91.4
May	73.7	45.4	117.6	71.7	50.3	66.7	128.6	87.4
June	74.4	43.6	115.2	69.1	48.3	68.8	128.6	88.0
July	89.6	52.4	111.2	68.4	49.9	68.1	128.6	92.3
August	90.3	51.1	109.7	68.8	48.2	70.9	128.6	92.8
September	87.1	55.4	110.7	69.5	47.7	71.6	128.6	90.3
October	86.5	55.6	103.8	68.4	46.1	68.8	128.6	84.2
November	79.5	48.6	88.0	64.3	38.9	65.4	128.6	80.0
December	89.6	49.6	75.1	63.6	37.8	64.0	128.6	79.2
Monthly average	83.6	49.7	109.6	70.4	48.1	68.9	131.0	89.9
1930, January	89.0	48.6	73.7	63.6	35.7	64.7	128.6	77.4
February	78.8	45.1	71.7	57.7	37.1	61.9	128.6	76.9
March	75.6	45.4	72.2	55.5	35.9	63.3	128.6	73.2
April	76.3	41.9	72.2	59.9	35.0	58.5	112.9	71.8
May	72.5	35.9	69.2	60.3	33.3	55.0	92.3	63.9
June	69.9	34.7	66.2	53.3	29.2	45.4	87.1	60.3
July	67.4	31.4	65.3	48.5	26.3	41.3	79.7	59.3
August	66.7	29.4	58.3	44.5	23.3	41.3	77.3	59.7
September	58.5	28.2	60.3	40.1	19.4	33.7	74.5	59.0
October	54.7	32.2	67.7	39.3	19.2	35.1	69.4	53.4
November	51.5	35.2	57.8	40.4	21.1	34.4	73.1	57.5
December	47.0	32.2	51.9	37.1	21.2	37.8	74.5	50.3
Monthly average	67.3	36.7	65.5	50.0	28.1	47.7	93.9	63.1
1931, January	43.2	34.2	48.4	37.5	19.5	39.2	71.2	51.9
February	44.5	32.7	47.0	40.4	18.0	37.8	70.3	52.3
March	42.6	31.9	42.5	40.1	18.1	35.8	71.2	53.9
April	45.1	32.2	42.5	37.5	15.1	31.7	67.9	50.0
May	45.8	29.4	46.0	34.2	15.2	31.7	62.7	46.2
June	42.6	32.9	47.9	33.1	14.9	34.4	58.1	46.6
July	39.4	37.4	46.0	34.2	14.9	33.0	55.7	49.8
August	33.7	36.4	41.0	26.5	12.6	35.1	52.7	51.2
September	33.7	35.2	39.5	23.9	11.9	32.3	50.5	49.1
October	37.5	35.2	38.6	23.5	11.4	31.7	49.0	45.3
November	40.7	33.7	39.5	23.9	10.9	32.3	47.4	45.4
December	36.2	28.2	42.5	23.2	10.9	27.5	47.6	42.5
Monthly average	40.4	33.3	43.5	31.5	14.5	33.5	58.7	48.7
1932, January	35.0	28.1	45.5	24.3	10.3	27.3	51.0	43.4
February	38.1	23.5	45.0	25.0	9.4	26.4	43.2	43.8
March	40.1	19.1	44.5	25.0	7.8	22.6	41.6	43.5
April	40.7	15.7	47.9	22.8	7.1	19.9	40.3	38.3
May	38.8	14.7	51.4	21.0	7.2	17.2	37.9	41.7
June	35.0	18.7	50.4	19.5	6.2	16.7	37.2	39.1
July	34.3	25.9	51.4	21.3	6.8	17.2	36.5	41.6
August	36.2	28.4	59.8	27.2	8.5	23.0	37.7	45.7
September	37.5	28.4	73.2	28.3	9.0	25.2	43.2	49.3
October	35.0	28.2	62.8	24.3	8.5	23.4	41.4	47.6
November	33.1	26.4	52.4	22.8	8.1	21.8	37.1	46.4
December	31.2	20.9	51.9	21.7	7.7	21.7	34.8	45.1
Monthly average	36.3	23.2	53.0	23.6	8.1	21.9	40.2	43.8
1933, January	32.0	..	48.4	22.8	7.3	18.2	34.6	45.2

[1] Imported red No. 2 at Liverpool. [2] 96° centrifugal c/f New York. [3] Santos No. 4 spot New York. [4] Middling upland, New York. [5] Smoked sheets, spot closing, New York. [6] Japanese 13–15, New York. [7] Electrolytic, New York. [8] Straits, New York.

9

The forces that were responsible for this recovery in prices, however, became exhausted in October, 1932, and in the last quarter of the year a new price decline set in, as may be seen from Table 3. Nevertheless prices remained above the low points for the year. In the first quarter of 1933 prices were well maintained and in some cases were considerably higher at the end of March, 1933, than in the summer of 1932.

The recovery of staple commodity prices and their ability to remain above the low points reached in 1932 are interpreted as indications that an equilibrium between supply and demand has been reached in the sense that current production is not in excess of consumption for the first time since

TABLE 4: WORLD STOCKS OF STAPLE COMMODITIES, END OF 1930, 1931, AND 1932

Source: Institut für Konjunkturforschung
In thousand metric tons

Commodity	1930	1931	1932	Percentage Decline (−) or Increase (+), 1931 to 1932
Wheat	14,873	16,570	16,130	− 3
Rye	998	806	415	−49
Sugar	8,810	9,393	9,682	+ 3
Coffee	1,930	2,214	1,835	−17
Cotton	2,245	2,312	2,393	+ 4
Silk	16	19	17	− 9
Rubber	488	627	621	− 1
Lead	102	151	180	+19
Zinc	325	307	263	−14
Tin	47	60	56	− 7
Coal	17,419	20,721	19,527	− 6

1925.[1] This interpretation of the price situation is supported by the decline in world stocks of staple commodities shown in Table 4. In the absence of concerted action on the part of the leading countries of the world to raise commodity prices, the price outlook, however, is not favorable. Commodity stocks are still abnormally high. Estimates of world production of agricultural staples in 1933 indicate no reduction in output. The cotton crop will be about the same as the record output of the preceding season. Restriction of sugar production under the International Sugar Agreement

[1] Institut für Konjunkturforschung, "Vierteljahrshefte zur Konjunkturforschung," Heft IV, Part A, Berlin, March, 1933, p. 249.

has not come up to expectations. In the case of minerals the existence of enormous production capacity and the absence of effective international agreements for production control are likely to exercise a depressing effect on prices through increase in production. Finally, the drift toward economic nationalism, as reflected in the Ottawa Agreements and in prohibitive tariff rates on imports of foodstuffs in many countries, must be regarded as depressing influences on world commodity prices.

TABLE 5: INDEX NUMBERS OF WHOLESALE PRICES,
7 COUNTRIES, 1931 TO 1933

Source: League of Nations

Year and Month	Great Britain, 1913 = 100	France, 1913 = 100	Germany, 1913 = 100	Italy, 1913 = 100	Japan, 1913 = 100	Sweden, 1913 = 100	United States, 1923 = 100
1931							
January	106.9	541	115.2	341.7	119.8	115	77.7
February	106.2	538	114.0	338.1	119.3	114	76.3
March	105.9	539	113.9	339.3	119.6	113	75.5
April	105.7	540	113.7	337.0	119.3	112	74.4
May	104.4	520	113.3	331.7	116.4	111	72.8
June	103.2	518	112.3	326.5	113.9	110	71.7
July	102.2	500	111.7	324.3	115.5	110	71.6
August	99.5	488	110.2	321.6	114.7	109	71.7
September	99.2	473	108.6	319.1	113.1	107	70.8
October	104.4	457	107.1	322.2	111.0	108	69.9
November	106.4	447	106.6	320.4	111.1	110	69.8
December	105.8	442	103.7	318.9	114.1	111	68.2
1932							
January	105.8	439	100.0	316.6	120.5	109	66.9
February	105.3	446	99.8	314.4	122.0	110	65.9
March	104.6	444	99.8	315.0	119.8	109	65.6
April	102.4	439	98.4	311.3	116.4	109	65.1
May	100.7	438	97.2	305.1	113.6	109	64.0
June	98.1	425	96.2	297.4	110.6	108	63.5
July	97.7	430	95.9	295.7	111.6	108	64.1
August	99.5	415	95.4	296.6	117.7	108	64.8
September	102.1	413	95.1	299.6	126.5	110	64.9
October	101.1	412	94.3	298.6	127.8	110	64.0
November	101.1	413	93.9	298.2	134.4	109	63.5
December	101.0	413	92.4	295.8	139.5	108	62.2
1933							
January	100.3	411	91.0	292.0	139.8	106	60.6
February	98.9	404	91.2	286.0	135.8	106	59.4
March	..	..	..	..	..	..	59.8

Index numbers of wholesale prices in the principal countries of the world are shown in Table 5. In the gold standard countries, the trend of prices through most of the year 1932 was downward. The slight recovery in some countries in the summer of 1932 was not maintained in the second half of the year, indicating that the increase in prices of raw materials and foodstuffs was more than offset by the decline in prices of finished manufactures. In the countries that have abandoned the gold standard, price deflation has been arrested.

TABLE 6: INDEX NUMBERS OF STERLING AND GOLD PRICES, SEPTEMBER, 1931, TO MARCH, 1933

Base, September 18, 1931 = 100

Source: The Economist

Date	Economist's Index of Sterling Prices	United States Prices, Irving Fisher Index
1931, September 30	107.8	98.7
November 11	110.3	99.3
November 25	109.1	98.3
December 30	108.9	96.1
1932, January 27	108.3	93.5
February 24	110.9	92.4
March 22	108.1	91.5
April 20	103.8	89.6
May 18	102.6	88.6
June 1	100.2	87.3
June 29	97.4	86.4
July 27	99.5	88.3
August 24	102.5	89.8
September 21	106.0	90.5
October 19	103.1	88.6
November 30	103.1	87.3
December 28	101.2	83.5
1933, January 25	101.3	80.5
February 22	99.2	79.9
March 22	99.0	82.1

Particular importance is attached to the movement of gold and sterling prices. From September, 1931, when Great Britain suspended gold payments, until June, 1932, gold prices declined, without any interruption, by about 13.6%. Immediately after the suspension of gold payments sterling prices, on the other hand, rose by 7.8% and remained relatively stable until March, 1932, when a decline set in, carrying the prices to a point below the September level in June, 1932. Between June and September, 1932, gold prices increased 4.7%, while sterling prices rose 8.8%. In the last quarter of the year, gold prices declined to the lowest point in the current business depression. Sterling prices declined only 4.5%, a more severe decline being averted by the depreciation in sterling, that is, the decline in the purchasing power of the pound sterling in terms of gold currencies. In the first quarter of 1933, the exchange value of the pound sterling remained stable, and gold and sterling prices moved downward. At the end of March, 1933, gold prices were about 17.9% lower than in the middle of September, 1931, while during the same period sterling prices declined only 1%. Table 6 shows the course of sterling and gold prices from September, 1931, to the end of March, 1933.

FOREIGN EXCHANGES

The movement of principal foreign exchanges in relation to the United States dollar from September, 1931, to March, 1933, is shown in Table 7. Following the suspension of gold payments in September, 1931, the pound sterling depreciated rapidly to about 69% of its par value in December, 1931. In the spring of 1932, sterling recovered to almost 80% of its par value, owing to the flow of short-term funds to London and the restoration of confidence in the financial stability of Great Britain. A considerable proportion of the funds withdrawn during the financial crisis in the summer of 1931 began to come back to London. In addition, sterling was strengthened by large exports of gold from India to the London financial market, from which it was later resold to other countries.

From April to December, 1932, sterling depreciated steadily, reaching the lowest point of $3.14 at the beginning of December. The flow of money to New York during the stock market boom in July and August was partly responsible for the decline. Sterling was under the usual seasonal pressure in the autumn, when the demand for dollar exchange on the part of British importers is very great. In the first part of December the uncertainty and confusion created by the dispute between the United States and Great Britain concerning the payment of the December instalment on the British war debt exerted a depressing influence on sterling exchange, but the apparent ease with which the payment was made out of the gold reserve of the Bank of England and the rapid accumulation of gold by the Bank in the early

TABLE 7: FOREIGN EXCHANGE RATES AND PERCENTAGES OF PAR VALUE, 7 COUNTRIES, SEPTEMBER, 1931, TO MARCH, 1933

Source: League of Nations; Computed by National Industrial Conference Board

Year and Month	Great Britain 1 £ = $4.8665		Sweden 1 Krona = $0.2680		Denmark 1 Krone = $0.2680		Canada 1 Canadian Dollar = $1.0000		Argentina 1 Peso = $0.9648		Australia 1 £ = $4.8665		Japan 1 Yen = $0.4985	
	Rate	Percentage of Par	Rate	Percentage of Par	Rate	Percentage of Par	Rate	Percentage of Par	Rate	Percentage of Par	Rate	Percentage of Par	Rate	Percentage of Par
1931														
September	$4.5313	93.1	$0.2609	97.4	$0.2526	94.3	$0.9625	96.3	$0.5969	61.9	$3.4789	71.5	$0.4934	99.0
October	3.8893	79.9	0.2311	86.2	0.2202	82.2	0.8910	89.1	0.5200	53.9	2.9860	61.4	0.4925	98.8
November	3.7199	76.4	0.2074	77.4	0.2067	77.1	0.8899	89.0	0.5884	61.0	2.8560	58.7	0.4930	98.9
December	3.3737	69.3	0.1871	69.8	0.1859	69.4	0.8271	82.7	0.5852	60.7	2.6850	55.2	0.4346	87.2
1932														
January	3.4312	70.5	0.1919	71.6	0.1888	70.4	0.8513	85.1	0.5827	60.4	2.7395	56.3	0.3599	72.2
February	3.4563	71.0	0.1929	72.0	0.1902	71.0	0.8729	87.3	0.5822	60.3	2.7595	56.7	0.3432	68.8
March	3.6393	74.8	0.1985	74.1	0.2001	74.7	0.8945	89.5	0.5829	60.4	2.9056	59.7	0.3216	64.5
April	3.7500	77.1	0.1909	71.2	0.2053	76.6	0.8988	89.9	0.5822	60.3	2.9940	61.5	0.3281	65.8
May	3.6751	75.5	0.1872	69.9	0.2007	74.9	0.8844	88.4	0.5832	60.4	2.9342	60.3	0.3197	64.1
June	3.6466	74.9	0.1870	69.8	0.1992	74.3	0.8674	86.7	0.5852	60.7	2.9115	59.8	0.3029	60.8
July	3.5496	72.9	0.1822	68.0	0.1920	71.6	0.8707	87.1	0.5856	60.7	2.8340	58.2	0.2745	55.1
August	3.4757	71.4	0.1785	66.6	0.1850	69.0	0.8755	87.6	0.5857	60.7	2.7750	57.0	0.2449	49.1
September	3.4711	71.3	0.1781	66.5	0.1798	67.1	0.9026	90.3	0.5859	60.7	2.7713	56.9	0.2363	47.4
October	3.3962	69.8	0.1753	65.4	0.1764	65.8	0.9123	91.2	0.5858	60.7	2.7115	55.7	0.2306	46.3
November	3.2753	67.3	0.1743	65.0	0.1706	63.7	0.8730	87.3	0.5858	60.7	2.6150	53.7	0.2062	41.4
December	3.2787	67.4	0.1791	66.8	0.1701	63.5	0.8660	86.6	0.5859	60.7	2.6177	53.8	0.2073	41.6
1933														
January	3.3614	69.1	0.1829	68.2	0.1691	63.1	0.8746	87.5	0.5858	60.7	2.6837	55.1	0.2074	41.6
February	3.4221	70.3	0.1827	68.2	0.1526	56.9	0.8351	83.5	0.5858	60.7	2.7322	56.1	0.2079	41.7
March	3.4574	71.0	0.1833	68.4	0.1540	57.5	0.8515	85.2	0.5858	60.7	2.7490	56.5	0.2110	42.3

part of 1933 produced a new advance in sterling, necessitating interference by the Government to prevent too rapid improvement in the pound.

The Government exercises some control over sterling exchange through the Exchange Equalization Fund. This Fund began to operate in July, 1932, with the object of preventing excessive speculative fluctuations in sterling. The Fund received from the British Treasury £150 million, largely in the form of treasury bills. The first step taken by the Fund was to take over from the Bank of England its holdings of foreign exchange—devisen. The operations of the Fund are secret. It does not issue a statement of its position. The reason for secrecy is the necessity of preventing the speculators from knowing the actual position of the Fund, but unfortunately this policy also keeps traders and investors in the dark concerning the real exchange value of the pound.

The British Government appears to be determined not to return to the gold standard, even at a new and lower parity, until financial, economic, and political conditions in the world become sufficiently stable to permit a smooth functioning of the international gold standard. This stand of the Government is supported by the leading bankers, industrialists, and economists of Great Britain. There is considerable disagreement among them, however, in regard to the immediate monetary policy of the Government. In the minds of many, the primary need of British industry and trade is a stable exchange. They agree that a rise in commodity prices is a prerequisite of world business recovery, but they doubt the ability of Great Britain alone to accomplish this end through monetary agency without the co-operation of other countries.

Another school of thought contends that the primary object of British monetary policy should be to raise sterling prices without regard to the monetary policies of other nations and the further depreciation of sterling exchange. In an address delivered on January 28, 1933, the Chancellor of the Exchequer showed little sympathy with this point of view. He pointed out that, if sterling prices moved upward, while gold prices were declining, other countries might de-

4

liberately depreciate their currencies, depriving Great Britain of any advantage from the low exchange value of sterling and inaugurating a period of extremely disturbing fluctuations in foreign exchange.

Since the abandonment of the gold standard in September, 1931, the Scandinavian exchanges have been linked more or less closely to sterling. Great Britain is the most important market for the exports of these countries. The suspension of gold payments in Great Britain, therefore, was followed automatically by the Scandinavian countries, and their exchanges have been kept at a slight discount to the pound.

The South American exchanges showed little or no fluctuations in 1932, owing to severe restrictions on dealings in foreign exchange. In Argentina the gold standard was suspended in December, 1929. Until October, 1931, the Argentine peso was allowed to depreciate without any official control. In that month, however, dealings in foreign exchange were placed under government control, and the exchange value of the peso was effectively pegged at 58.5 cents, or about 40% below its par value. Brazil did not legally adopt the gold standard after the World War, but at the end of 1926 the milreis was stabilized at 11.96 cents. In December, 1929, the milreis went below its gold parity and continued to decline throughout 1930 and 1931. In January, 1932, the milreis was quoted at 6.16 cents, or approximately 50% of its par value. In the second half of 1932 and the first quarter of 1933 the nominal exchange value of the milreis has been maintained at 7.6 cents. In Chile foreign exchange control was introduced in September, 1931, but the gold standard was not suspended until April, 1932. Since that time the nominal value of the Chilean peso has been 6.0 cents, or about 50% below its par value. In Colombia the gold standard was suspended in November, 1931, but by means of strict foreign exchange control the Colombian peso was maintained at about 98% of its gold parity until March, 1933, when it depreciated to about 89% of par.[1]

In the Far East, Japan suspended the gold standard in December, 1931, and introduced foreign exchange control in

[1] Actual market rates of Brazilian, Chilean, and Colombian exchanges, however, were considerably lower than the nominal rate.

September, 1932. Throughout 1932 the Japanese yen depreciated rapidly, reaching the low point at the end of the year, when it was quoted at about 20 cents, as compared with the par value of 49.85 cents. In the first quarter of 1933 the exchange value of the yen remained stable, with a slight tendency to appreciate. The depreciation of the yen to about 41% of its par value was not accompanied by suspension of debt payments to foreign creditors and is felt with extreme severity by the Japanese companies that borrowed abroad rather heavily in the years before 1930. The burden of their foreign debt service has been more than doubled by the decline in the exchange value of the yen.

China is on a silver standard, and the exchange value of its currency is determined by the price of silver. The average rate of exchange of the Shanghai tael in terms of United States dollars was $0.5842 in 1929; $0.4182 in 1930; $0.3112 in 1931; and $0.3065 in 1932. The low point in the exchange value of the tael was reached in December, 1932. In the first quarter of 1933 the Chinese exchange remained fairly stable, as a result of the stability in the price of silver.

Australia suspended the gold standard in September, 1929. The average rate of exchange of the Australian pound was $4.586 in 1930; $3.515 in 1931; and $2.780 in 1932, as compared with the par value of $4.866. Since the suspension of the gold standard in Great Britain the exchange value of the Australian pound has moved in sympathy with the pound sterling, being at a discount of 20.2% throughout the year 1932.

Canada suspended the gold standard in October, 1931. Throughout 1932 and the first quarter of 1933 the exchange value of the Canadian dollar moved between 80% and 90% of its par value. Canada has not introduced government control of foreign exchange transactions, but shipments of gold from Canada are not allowed except under license.

The German, Polish, Czechoslovak, Hungarian, and Rumanian exchanges were maintained at their parities with gold by means of more or less drastic restrictions on foreign exchange transactions. In Jugoslavia and Austria the gold standard was not legally abandoned, but the exchange was allowed to depreciate to about 80% of par value. Czechoslovakia made punctually all payments to foreign creditors, including the December instalment on the war debt to the United States, assisted by a loan from France of 600 million francs. With the exception of the December debt payment to the United States, Poland was able to fulfill all her foreign debt obligations without undue strain and with a minimum of interference with foreign exchange transactions. Hungary, Jugoslavia, Rumania, Bulgaria, and Greece are in a state of insolvency in regard to their foreign debt obligations. The value of their exchanges is purely nominal.

The German reichsmark has been kept at parity with gold by means of an extremely drastic system of foreign exchange control and with the help of foreign creditors, who have agreed to a gradual liquidation of their short-term loans to Germany. Removal of exchange restrictions would undoubtedly be followed by a marked depreciation in German exchange.

French, Belgian, Dutch, Swiss, and Italian exchanges were kept at their gold parities throughout 1932 and in the first quarter of 1933 without any official control of foreign exchange or gold movements. In Italy, however, exchange transactions are controlled unofficially by the Italian Federation of Credit and Insurance.

Prospects for Currency Stabilization

If the recommendations of the Gold Delegation of the League of Nations and of the Preparatory Committee of Experts of the International Economic Conference are regarded as representing the attitude of the principal world powers, a restoration of the international gold standard should be expected. Both of these groups of experts recommend a general return to the gold standard, but they recognize that the new standard must be a managed standard. The object of this management would be to bring about the reassertion of the forces making for proper distribution of the world gold supply, which operated automatically before the World War or that were made to operate by the financial power of Great Britain. The Gold Delegation specifically says, in its 1932 report, that not only should gold movements not be prevented from causing a rise in prices in the countries receiving gold and a fall in prices in the countries losing gold, but that their working should be reinforced by changes in the discount rate and open market operations, in order to correct the disequilibria of which the gold movements give evidence, and which cannot be corrected by those movements.

If this recommendation of the Gold Delegation were accepted, the countries that at the present time have excessive stocks of gold would deliberately inflate their prices and make commodity exports more difficult, while countries with inadequate gold reserves would further deflate their prices in order to increase their commodity exports. The carrying out of this policy would raise serious difficulties and would require specific international agreements to guard against recriminations between the countries losing gold and those gaining gold. It would be, for example, necessary to define what degree of inflation or deflation is required to bring about adequate pressure on outward or inward movements of gold. The Gold Delegation did not indicate what machinery would have to be created to insure an effective control of international gold distribution.

The Gold Delegation suggested, furthermore, that after the restoration of the gold standard the object of central bank policy should be to control the changes in the purchasing power of gold, that is, the fluctuations in commodity prices. What action should be taken to accomplish this desirable end was not explicitly stated. The Delegation did not recommend the adoption of a compensated money unit, the gold content of which would be increased or decreased in accordance with the downward or upward movement of prices. This apparently was regarded as practically impossible. What the members of the Delegation had in mind was "a relative, but not an absolute, stability of wholesale commodity prices as measured by their movements over a long series of years." Unfortunately they did not make clear what they understood by this price relativity, nor did they suggest a mechanism by means of which it could be attained.

Finally, the Gold Delegation recommended specifically that the minimum ratios between central bank gold reserves and their sight liabilities be reduced from their present high levels, in order to "free the hands of the Central Banks by enlarging the free margin of their gold reserves which they can use for international payments without endangering the legal minimum ratio."

The Committee of Experts of the International Economic Conference, in its report issued in January, 1933, accepted the proposals of the Gold Delegation in regard to the desirability of restoring an international gold standard, but laid greater emphasis on the necessity of taking immediate action to increase commodity prices and to bring about a more uniform distribution of gold. The Committee urged a policy of cheap money in the gold-standard countries and warned the countries off the gold standard against a competitive depreciation of their currencies. In the opinion of the Committee no return to the gold standard is possible until trade obstructions in the form of import quotas, licensing systems, foreign exchange restrictions, and excessive tariffs are removed. These restrictions, however, cannot be removed so long as the withdrawal of short-term foreign credits represents a threat to the financial stability of many debtor countries, so long as the burden of interest payments on the long-term foreign debts imposes an excessive strain on the balance of payments of the debtor countries, and so long as the various countries find it necessary to prevent the flight of domestic capital.

A particularly important suggestion of the Committee of Experts is that concerning the level at which the currencies of the countries with depleted reserves should be stabilized. The new gold parities "should be such as to be consistent with a favorable balance of payments and so attract an adequate reserve without undue effort." In other words, the return to the gold standard must be preceded by a careful study of the balance of international payments of each country at the present time and of the probable influences on that balance in the future.

This observation is of fundamental importance. The working of the gold standard in the future will depend to a large extent on the levels at which the various currencies are stabilized in relation to gold. In devaluating its currency, that is, in reducing the gold content of the monetary unit, each country will undoubtedly attempt to choose the new gold parity with a view to strengthening its international position, favoring its exports, and protecting its domestic market from foreign competition. The Committee of Experts states that each country must be free to decide when and under what conditions it will stabilize its currency. In theory the liberty of a country to choose any monetary standard it wishes cannot be denied. In practice, however, this liberty is limited by the necessity of avoiding retaliation on the part of other countries. No country has a monopoly on currency depreciation. Some countries, to be sure, may benefit more than others by depreciating the external purchasing power of their currencies; an important creditor country, for example, that derives a large income from foreign investments may benefit less than a debtor country concerned primarily with increasing its surplus of exports. But that weapon is available to all countries, and in the absence of international co-operation its use might lead to competitive currency depreciation that would be ruinous for all countries.

Obviously, therefore, in devaluating its currency each country must consider the interests of the other countries. In stating that the new gold parities should be consistent with a favorable balance of payments in order to attract adequate reserves without undue effort, the Committee of Experts referred to the countries whose reserves are seriously depleted at the present time. Under normal conditions, however, the accumulation of adequate reserves by these countries could be accomplished in a relatively short period, especially if the creditor countries found it possible to resume foreign lending. It is essential, therefore, that, as soon as the reserves of these countries are replenished, imports of gold should cease and international payments be balanced by imports of goods and services. Thus, while the creditor countries with abundant gold reserves should in their own interest co-operate with the countries having inadequate supplies of gold in stabilizing their currencies in such a manner as to promote a temporary inflow of gold, they should expect them to permit the inflow of gold to exercise its normal influence on internal prices according to the rules of the gold standard after their reserves rise to the desired level. In theory this arrangement looks equitable and simple. Its practical execution, however, would be fraught with great difficulties. It would be extremely difficult, in the first place, to decide to what point the gold reserves of the individual countries should be built up and, in the second place, to obtain the consent of the different countries to prevent the inflow of gold after their reserves have reached the amount agreed upon as adequate.

The problem of currency devaluation is even more difficult in the case of such economically powerful countries as the United States and Great Britain. The battle between the dollar and the pound appears unreal to the average citizen, but its effects are felt throughout the world, and its outcome will strongly influence the future economic welfare of the two countries. The United States and Great Britain are the principal creditor countries of the world. Great Britain is the greatest market for American exports, one of the largest exporters to the United States, and one of the leading competitors of the United States in the world markets. Neither country can afford, therefore, to permit the other to obtain even a temporary advantage through depreciation of the currency or through its stabilization at a point that would give advantage to one country over the other in international trade. Stabilization of the two currencies at a lower gold parity could be accomplished arbitrarily and by independent action, but this policy would be dangerous to the country that tied its currency to gold without knowing at what level the other country would decide to stabilize.

If the exchange value of the pound were stabilized at a point where its external purchasing power would be appreciably lower than its internal purchasing power, while the dollar were stabilized at or above its internal purchasing power, British exporters would be favored at the expense of American exporters, and all countries of the world would find it more profitable to sell in the United States and to buy in Great Britain than the other way around.

Aside from the factors of international trade competition, currency devaluation must take into account the social and economic conditions within each country. A country like the United States, where the value of foreign trade is only a small, although important, fraction of its total business, may find it necessary to devalue its currency as a result of purely domestic needs and regardless of the condition of its balance of international payments. As a matter of fact, the balance of payments of the United States was favorable at the time when the gold standard was abandoned, but the necessity of reversing the process of domestic deflation led to the suspension of gold payments in order to permit the Government to deal with the domestic situation without fearing a panicky flight of funds to foreign countries for safe keeping. For the same reason, in returning to the gold standard on a new and lower parity, the United States may be guided by considerations of a purely domestic character to a much larger extent than a country like Great Britain, which must buy most of its foodstuffs and raw materials from abroad.

In addition to currency devaluation, it is proposed that, in order to ensure rising commodity prices, the governments of at least some of the leading countries should agree on a program of increasing the purchasing power in the hands of the consumers by undertaking the construction of extensive public works, financed by long-term loans.

In the field of international finance it may be desirable to establish some form of co-operation among the leading creditor countries to bring about a resumption of international financing and facilitate the removal of foreign exchange restrictions that are now practised by about forty countries. This co-operation may take the form of a special International Credit Institute, which would function either as an independent body or would be administered by the Bank for International Settlements. The Institute could derive its funds either from the Central Banks or from private sources. The function of the Institute would be to extend new loans to the debtor countries rather than to refinance the outstanding obligations of a long-term or short-term character. The task of liquidating the old short-term credits that may now be "frozen" or regulated by standstill agreements and of reducing the service of long-term debts that may or may not be in default at the present time should properly be undertaken by the creditors and debtors them-

5

selves, but an International Credit Institute should be of immense value in facilitating amicable settlements, by giving impartial advice to the interested parties on matters relating to the international financial position of the various countries. After the present emergency is passed, the Institute could serve ias an international advisory body on all matters connected with the international movement of funds.

This brief analysis of some of the aspects of international financial reconstruction is sufficient to show the magnitude of the task facing the World Economic Conference. If the political difficulties are added to the economic problems, the prospects do not appear encouraging at the present time. The question of disarmament and security has been discussed for sixteen months by the Disarmament Conference at Geneva, but it cannot be said that any genuine progress has been made toward its solution or that a satisfactory solution is in sight. Economic developments, however, will not wait until the political difficulties are solved, and it may be that a revival of business and trade would lessen the political tension. With idle time on their hands, people are prone to turn their attention to politics. Full employment and satisfactory pay checks might ease the political tension, cool off passions, and promote good will and a spirit of liberalism.

In the opinion of many students of politics and economics, the problem that faces the world is one of saving the present civilization from collapse. The road to salvation lies in a revival of industrial and trade activity, and it is generally agreed that this revival in turn requires higher commodity prices. The immediate task of the World Economic Conference is to secure the co-operation of the governments to increase commodity prices up to a level that will provide employment for the millions of workers who are now unemployed or are working short-time. What this price level should be cannot be determined at the present time. For the same reason it is impossible to determine the extent to which the various currencies should be depreciated in terms of gold. Currency and price stabilization, therefore, is a problem of the future and should perhaps be the subject of a later World Economic Conference. The forthcoming Conference should be considered a success if it leads to the adoption of general economic policies for increasing the level of commodity prices and of specific policies for the prevention of wide fluctuations in exchange rates and the elimination of existing restrictions on foreign exchange transactions and foreign trade.

CURRENCY DEPRECIATION AND BUSINESS ACTIVITY

The immediate and perhaps the most important effect of currency depreciation was to arrest and to reverse the downward trend of commodity prices. As may be seen in Table 5, the countries with depreciated currencies have had a rising or a relatively stable commodity price level, while the countries that have remained on the gold standard have experienced further drastic deflation in commodity prices. This development was to be expected, as the natural result of currency depreciation is an advance in prices. It is more difficult to appraise the effects of currency depreciation on industrial and trade activity. Have the volume of industrial production and the value of foreign trade been better maintained in the countries with depreciated currencies than in those that have remained on the gold standard?

There is no satisfactory and internationally comparable measure of industrial production. A number of countries collect data relating to the physical volume of production in the various manufacturing and mining industries. The results of this investigation are published on a monthly basis in the form of index numbers of production. These index numbers do not show the physical volume of production, but only the changes in industrial activity. In making comparisons of the relative changes in production as between one country and another, it is necessary to remember that the index numbers differ materially in regard to the number and character of the industries covered and the methods of calculation.

Index numbers of industrial production for 6 countries from 1930 to 1933 are shown in Table 8. Three of these countries—the United States, Germany, and France—have maintained the gold parity of their exchanges throughout the

period covered in the table. The other three countries—
England, Sweden, and Japan—have suspended the gold

TABLE 8: INDEX NUMBERS OF PRODUCTION, 6 COUNTRIES,
1930 TO 1933

Base, 1928 = 100

Source: League of Nations

Year and Month	United States	Germany	France	England	Sweden¹	Japan
1930						
Jan.	95.5	99.5	113.4		110.2	..
Feb.	96.4	97.8	112.6	105.1	108.3	..
Mar.	93.7	97.3	113.4		104.6	..
April	93.7	94.8	113.4		102.3	..
May	91.9	93.0	113.4	97.7	95.4	..
June	88.3	88.9	113.4		97.2	..
July	83.8	86.5	111.0		96.3	..
August	81.1	86.6	109.4	94.2	96.3	..
Sept.	81.1	85.5	107.9		93.5	..
Oct.	79.3	84.4	107.1		93.5	..
Nov.	77.5	84.7	106.3	93.8	92.6	..
Dec.	75.7	82.5	105.5		92.6	..
1931						
Jan.	75.7	77.6	104.7		77.8	..
Feb.	77.5	74.8	104.7	90.0	81.5	..
Mar.	78.4	76.5	103.9		82.4	..
April	79.3	78.2	103.1		88.9	..
May	78.4	77.6	101.6	87.1	83.3	..
June	74.8	78.9	99.2		85.2	100.1
July	73.9	78.2	96.9		88.0	105.6
Aug.	70.3	72.8	95.3	84.6	89.8	103.2
Sept.	68.5	71.1	93.7		88.0	103.6
Oct.	65.8	66.7	92.1		90.4	103.4
Nov.	65.8	66.4	89.8	92.2	93.3	102.0
Dec.	66.7	63.8	87.4		97.1	101.7
1932						
Jan.	64.9	61.9	82.7		93.3	95.7
Feb.	62.2	62.6	78.7	90.0	91.3	99.7
Mar.	60.4	61.4	77.2		96.2	107.7
April	56.8	61.0	74.8		83.7	104.3
May	54.1	62.2	74.0	89.4	87.5	106.6
June	53.2	60.9	73.2		76.9	103.6
July	52.3	60.4	72.4		71.2	106.5
Aug.	54.1	58.5	73.2	82.7	77.9	106.0
Sept.	59.5	60.3	74.0		81.7	109.1
Oct.	60.4	60.7	74.8		79.8	113.0
Nov.	58.6	62.3	76.4	89.6	82.7	118.5
Dec.	59.5	61.9	77.2		83.7	124.5
1933						
Jan.	57.7	62.2	78.7	..	82.7	..
Feb.	..	62.5	81.1	..	85.6	..

¹ Revised index since October, 1932.

standard. Examination of the figures shows immediately
that the volume of production in the gold standard countries

was sharply reduced in 1932, as compared with 1931. In England and Sweden industrial activity was well maintained, while in Japan it showed an actual increase. In the case of Japan, where a marked increase in activity took place in 1932, the improvement should not be ascribed entirely to currency depreciation, since the national economy of Japan in 1932 was dominated in a large measure by the military operations in Manchuria and China. Nevertheless, the evidence presented by the statistics of the physical volume of production points to the conclusion that the countries that have arrested the process of deflation by divorcing their currencies from gold have been able to maintain a more satisfactory level of industrial activity than the countries that have adhered to the gold standard.

Further evidence of a better situation in the countries that have gone off the gold standard is found in the figures of the value of exports and imports shown in the following table:

Country	Percentage Decline from 1931 to 1932	
	Exports	Imports
Gold-standard countries		
United States	33.5	36.7
France	35.3	29.3
Germany	40.2	30.5
Italy	31.5	28.2
Poland	42.2	40.9
Switzerland	42.6	22.9
Countries off the gold standard		
Great Britain	29.2	36.9
Sweden	38.5	40.6
Norway	12.1	42.3
Canada	26.9	34.7
Argentina	22.7	37.7
Brazil	23.8	19.8
Australia	16.8	5.6
Japan	32.3	36.1

The decline in the value of exports of the gold standard countries from 1931 to 1932 was, with few exceptions, greater than the reduction of exports of the countries that have depreciated their currencies. While, of course, in a number of countries with depreciated currencies, shown in Table 1, exports have declined as much as, or more than, those of the gold standard countries, the fact that stands out most clearly, and that is of real significance, is that the countries with depreciated currencies have been able to increase their share of world exports at the expense of the countries that have remained on the gold standard. In addition, currency depreciation has made it possible for these countries to improve their balance of merchandise trade by effecting a reduction in the value of imports larger than the decline in the value of exports.

II

CONDITIONS IN INDIVIDUAL COUNTRIES

GREAT BRITAIN

The violent contraction of industrial and trade activity that occurred in 1930 and 1931 was definitely arrested in 1932. The total physical volume of production in 1932 was approximately the same as in the preceding year. The level of activity in the iron and steel, textile, chemical, and gas and electricity industries was greater in 1932 than in 1931, the increase being particularly marked in the production of textiles. The output of coal in 1932 was about 5.0% less than in 1931, while the activity in the shipbuilding and engineering trades showed a decline of 7.3%.[1] The Board of Trade index numbers of production are shown in Table 9.

TABLE 9: INDEX NUMBERS OF PRODUCTION, GREAT BRITAIN, 1930 TO 1932

Base, 1924 = 100

Source: Board of Trade Journal

Industry	1930	1931	1932	Percentage Increase + or Decrease − from 1931 to 1932
Mines and quarries....................	91.3	81.6	77.5	− 5.0
Iron and steel and manufactures thereof	88.8	65.9	66.2	+ 0.5
Non-ferrous metals...................	119.1	100.1	96.3	− 3.8
Engineering and shipbuilding.........	116.6	94.9	88.0	− 7.3
Textiles..............................	79.5	77.0	85.1	+10.5
Chemical and allied trades...........	99.3	95.2	97.7	+ 2.6
Leather and boots and shoes.........	101.4	99.3	96.4	− 2.9
Food, drink, and tobacco............	104.9	103.7	97.6	− 5.9
Gas and electricity..................	138.7	142.4	146.1	+ 2.6
Total........................	103.2	93.7	93.1	− 0.6

Balance of International Payments

The value of merchandise exports declined from £454.5 million, $2,061 million, in 1931 to £416.0 million, $1,459

[1] "The Board of Trade Journal," London, February 23, 1933, pp. 290–291.

million, in 1932. During the same period the value of imports declined from £861.3 million, $3,906 million, to £703.1 million, $2,465 million. The surplus of commodity imports over commodity exports amounted to £286.9 million in 1932, $1,006 million, as compared with £406.8 million, $1,845 million, in 1931.

The enormous reduction in the surplus of commodity imports in 1932 has materially improved the British balance of international payments, as may be seen from Table 10. In 1931 Great Britain had a deficit of £104 million, $472 million, on account of current international transactions. This deficit had to be met by the sale of British foreign assets. In 1932 the adverse balance was reduced to £59 million, $207 million. This sum, however, includes £29 million paid to the United States Government in December, 1932, on account of the British war debt. In making the payment in gold, the British Government stated that it was to be regarded as a capital payment to be taken into account in a final settlement of the British debt to the United States. Since the balance of payments prepared by the Board of Trade covers only current credit and debit transactions,

TABLE 10: BALANCE OF INTERNATIONAL PAYMENTS, GREAT BRITAIN, 1930 TO 1932

Source: Board of Trade Journal

In millions

Item	1930		1931		1932	
	Pound Sterling	Dollars	Pound Sterling	Dollars	Pound Sterling	Dollars
Debits						
Surplus of commodity imports[1]....	386	1,878	408	1,850	289	1,013
Credits						
Net income from shipping........	105	511	80	363	70	245
Net income from foreign investments	220	1,070	170	771	140	491
Net receipts from short interest and commission....................	55	267	30	136	30	105
Net receipts from other sources....	15	73	10	45	15	53
Excess of government receipts from overseas......................	19	92	14	63	25[2]	88
Total credits...............	414	2,013	304	1,379	255	894
Total debits (−) or credit (+)....	+28	+136	−104	−472	−59	−207

[1] Including silver transactions.
[2] Debit.

other than the lending and repayment of capital, the American debt payment should not have been included. If this principle is adopted, the excess of payments over receipts in 1932 is reduced to £30 million, $105.2 million, showing an improvement of £74 million, $259.0 million, as compared with the situation in 1931.

The trend of merchandise trade in the first two months of 1933 indicates that the surplus of commodity imports will be further reduced in the current year. The value of exports in the first two months of 1933 was £65.8 million, $225 million, and that of imports, £103.0 million, $352 million. As compared with the corresponding period of 1932 imports showed a decline of £29.4 million, $101 million, while exports were reduced only £6.1 million, $21 million.[1]

Public Finance

In the fiscal year ended March 31, 1932, Great Britain was the only country in the world that had succeeded in balancing its national budget. The improvement that has taken place in the economic position of Great Britain since the summer of 1931 is ascribed largely to the energetic measures taken by the British Government in balancing the national accounts. Preliminary estimates for the fiscal year ended March 31, 1933, indicate that there will be an approximate balance between revenues and expenditures, with perhaps a slight deficit. Total revenue in 1932/33 was placed in the budgetary estimates of the Chancellor of the Exchequer at £766.8 million, and total expenditure, at £766.0 million. On the basis of the actual figures up to March 11, 1933, it appears that total receipts will be about £687.0 million, or about £10 million less than total expenditures.

The balancing of the budget was materially assisted by increased revenues from customs duties. Even the advocates of free trade recognize the significant contribution that the customs revenues are making to the public treasury. The revenue from customs duties is estimated at about £169 millions in 1932/33, as compared with £174.6 million in the preceding fiscal year.

[1] "The Economist," London, March 18, 1933, p. 577.

Employment, Wages, and Cost of Living

The volume of unemployment increased in 1932. The average number of insured persons employed in 1932 was 9,352,000, as compared with 9,421,000 in 1931. Unemployment among insured workers averaged 21.3% in 1931 and 22.1% in 1932. The increase in unemployment was greatest in the building, mining, and jute and lace industries. The level of employment in the cotton, silk, chemical, pottery, glass, motor, and leather manufacturing industries, on the other hand, was appreciably higher in 1932 than in 1931.[1]

The depreciation in the exchange value of the pound sterling after the abandonment of the gold standard was not accompanied by an increase in wage rates. The index number of wages, base 1924 = 100, declined from 98.5 in the first quarter of 1931 to 97.0 in the last quarter of 1931, and to 95.5 in the last quarter of 1932. From 1924 to 1930 the index number of wages fluctuated between 102.5 in the second quarter of 1925 and 99.0 in the last quarter of 1930.[2] The rigidity of wage rates, enforced by the political power of the trade unions, was one of the main difficulties of Great Britain after the return to the gold standard in 1925. The decline in gold prices required a downward adjustment in the costs of production, including the cost of labor. Owing to the opposition of the trade unions, however, manufacturers were unable to reduce the rates of wages paid to organized workers. The depreciation in sterling exchange, therefore, has given an immediate and important advantage to British manufacturers, by cheapening the money with which their fixed wage commitments are paid, and this advantage will continue as long as British money wages do not increase.

The pressure for wage increases in not likely to become severe until the cost of living begins to rise, that is, until the purchasing power of wages begins to decline. The index number of the cost of living, base 1924 = 100, declined from 86.2 in the first quarter of 1931 to 83.9 in the last quarter of that year and to 81.8 in the last quarter of 1932.[3]

[1] "The Economist," February 18, 1933, p. 12.
[2] Supplement to the "Ministry of Labour Gazette," February, 1933.
[3] Idem.

GERMANY

The improvement that was noted in the economic position of Germany after the Lausanne Agreement in July, 1932, was arrested by the extraordinary political developments in connection with the assumption of power and responsibility by the National Socialist Party of Adolf Hitler. The change in government, however, was not accompanied by a new decline in business activity. If the movement of security prices is taken as a fair indicator of business confidence in the new régime, the conclusion must be drawn that the elimination of the Reichstag and the assumption of almost dictatorial powers by the Hitler Cabinet have been welcomed in German business and financial circles.[1] The index number of stock prices on the Berlin Stock Exchange, base, 1927–29 = 100, increased from 43.8 at the end of 1932 to 50.9 on March 25, 1933. On July 1, 1932, the index stood at 30.0.

The announcement made by the government and the new President of the Reichsbank, Dr. Schacht, that there would be no radical changes in monetary policy and the realization that the new régime would not attempt any adventures in the conduct of foreign affairs were no doubt largely responsible for the renewal of confidence reflected in the rising prices of securities in the first quarter of 1933.

Less satisfactory, on the other hand, from the point of view of the export industries of Germany—iron and steel, machinery, electrical equipment, chemical, and coal—is the commercial policy of the new Government, which aims to make Germany practically independent of foreign countries in regard to agricultural products. The policy of economic nationalism is bound to lead, and has already led, to the adoption of retaliatory measures by the agricultural countries of Europe that supply Germany with most of her imports of butter, eggs, poultry, bacon, lard, wheat, and so on.

The reduction of German exports from 1,606 million reichsmarks, $382 million, in the first three months of 1932 to 1,190 million reichsmarks, $284 million, in the correspond-

[1] It should be observed, however, that the advent of the Hitler Government was not accompanied by any improvement in the prices of German securities quoted on the foreign stock exchanges. In the early part of May, 1933, German security prices declined rather sharply.

ing period of 1933 is a most unsatisfactory development. Although the decline in exports cannot be attributed solely to the retaliatory measures adopted by the agricultural countries of Europe—Rumania, Jugoslavia, Czechoslovakia, Denmark, the Netherlands, and Poland—it is certain that a recovery in German exports, which is essential in order both to provide full employment to the industrial population and to avoid default on foreign debts, will be extremely difficult if Germany does not find a way of concluding satisfactory trade agreements with the countries that have for years looked to Germany as the best market for their surplus agricultural production and have been Germany's best customers.[1]

Balance of International Payments

At the end of March, 1932, the Federal Statistical Office of Germany published a new estimate of the German balance of international payments in 1932. The net income from merchandise trade and from services rendered to foreigners is estimated at 1,400 million reichsmarks, $333 million, while the net deficit on account of foreign debt service is placed at 1,100 million reichsmarks, $262 million, leaving a balance of 300 million reichsmarks, $71 million, for debt repayment. The total amount of debt repayment in 1932 is estimated at 1,200 million reichsmarks, $286 million. The foreign exchange required for this repayment was made available (1) through the return of capital from abroad and repayment of export credits granted to foreign customers in 1931, amounting together to at least 400 million reichsmarks, $95 million; (2) through the reduction in foreign assets of German banks estimated at 250 million reichsmarks, $60 million; (3) through the conversion of short-term loans into long-term loans amounting to about 100 million reichsmarks, $24 million; and (4) through the reduction in gold and foreign exchange reserves of 300 million reichsmarks, $71 million.

The most significant item in the new official estimate of the balance of payments is the income from services rendered to foreigners. The gross income from shipping services, tourist expenditures, and transit shipments in 1932 is esti-

[1] In May, 1933, it was announced in Berlin that a partial moratorium on Germany's foreign indebtedness would be declared before the end of the month.

mated at 749 million reichsmarks, $178 million, and the net income, at 380 million reichsmarks, $91 million. There was also a net income of 14 million reichsmarks, $3 million, from motion picture royalties. But there was a net deficit of 55 million reichsmarks, $13 million, from insurance transactions and postal services, leaving a net income from all services rendered to foreigners of 339 million reichsmarks, $81 million.

The importance of the income from services rendered to foreigners to the German balance of international payments has been often underestimated. The new estimate of the German Government shows that the ability of Germany to fulfill her foreign debt obligations in 1933 will be strongly influenced by the extent to which foreigners find it advantageous to use German ships and to visit German resorts during the summer season. In 1932 the income of the German shipping companies from carrying foreign passengers amounted to 135 million reichsmarks, and the income from tourist expenditures is estimated at 100 million reichsmarks.

Prices, Wages, and the Cost of Living

Wholesale prices continued to decline throughout 1932, but the rate of decline slowed down in the second half of the year. In February, 1933, the index number of wholesale prices, base 1913 = 100, increased to 91.2 from the low point of 91.0 reached in January, 1933. This was the first increase in wholesale prices since July, 1930. Raw material prices reached the low point in July, 1932, increased slightly during the summer, and remained relatively stable during the rest of the year. The firmness of raw material prices was due to higher prices paid for imported products. The index number of agricultural prices declined from 92.1 in January, 1932, to 80.9 in January, 1933. During the same period prices of finished manufactures declined from 125.2 to 113.0, while prices of raw materials decreased only from 92.2 to 87.1. The relative stability of prices of raw materials of foreign origin is viewed as an unfavorable development from the point of view of German export industries. Continuation of the same tendency, without an increase in the prices of German export products, would increase costs of production in Germany and impede exports.

The reduction in wages paid to organized industrial workers that began in January, 1931, continued without interruption in 1932. The actual hourly rate of wages paid to skilled male workers under trade union agreements declined from the post-war maximum of 24.5 cents in December, 1930 to 19.0 cents in December, 1932, or 22.4%. During the same period the index number of the cost of living, base 1913–14 = 100, declined from 141.6 to 118.4. Further reductions in labor costs may be expected, but it is not believed that the export industries of Germany are likely to receive substantial relief from this source.

There are, however, two important items in the cost of production that could be reduced considerably under a strong central government. In the opinion of German industrial leaders, heavy taxation and excessive social charges, in the form of contributions to various social insurance institutions imposed upon German industry since the World War by the various socialist governments, have deprived the German industry of most of the benefits of rationalization, of improvements in the efficiency of production and distribution, accomplished since the stabilization of the currency in 1924. The present Government has not yet announced its policy in regard to the existing system of social legislation. The opinion is widely held that an attempt will be made to break the power of organized labor, but it is not known how far the Government will go in restoring a greater measure of elasticity to the economic system in line with the principles of private enterprise and operation of industry for profit. As a matter of fact, the most confusing aspect of the German situation is the lack of any accurate information concerning the real relationship between the Government and the representatives of German industry and trade.

Money and Credit

In the course of 1932 the Reichsbank was able to reduce its discount rate from 7% to 4%. Call money rates were reduced during the year from 7.87% to 4.97%, and 30-day money rates declined from 8.75% to 5.75%. The interest on overdrafts, including commission, was reduced by the commercial banks from 10% to 7%. During the last decade before the World War, the Reichsbank discount rate and the rates on overdrafts were as a rule higher than at the present time. The short-term interest rates, however, are still too high when compared with those prevailing in the principal money markets of the world. These rates in Germany are about three times higher than those in London, New York, Paris, Zurich, and Amsterdam.

The note circulation of the Reichsbank declined from 4,776 million reichsmarks, $1,138 million, at the beginning of 1932 to 3,197 million reichsmarks, $762 million, on March 23, 1933. During the same period the holdings of gold declined from 984 million reichsmarks, $234 million, to 727 million reichsmarks, $173 million, while the holdings of foreign exchange were reduced from 172 million reichsmarks, $41 million, to 122 million reichsmarks, $29 million. At the end of 1929, the gold reserve of the Reichsbank was 2,283 million reichsmarks, $544 million, and the holdings of foreign exchange were 404 million reichsmarks, $96 million.

The commercial and financial relations of Germany with the rest of the world are controlled strictly by the Government. Default on short-term credits granted to Germany by foreign financial and business institutions has been avoided by the conclusion of standstill credit agreements, under which foreign creditors have agreed to a gradual and orderly liquidation of their short-term advances. The régime of severe restrictions on foreign exchange transactions, which prevents normal exchange of goods between Germany and the rest of the world, cannot be removed so long as the danger of credit withdrawals constitutes a threat to the stability of German currency. Conversion of short-term credits into long-term loans, which has been urged as a necessary measure by all international conferences that have met in the last two years, would provide a solution of this difficulty. This solution, however, is impossible at the present time, on account of the dislocation of international capital markets and the uncertain condition of political affairs in Germany.

There can be no doubt that from both the economic and the political point of view the present economic situation in Germany is critical. Without an improvement in business and a revival of international trade under more normal conditions, the strain on the international balance of payments of Germany may become so great as to require a complete or partial suspension of payments on her foreign debts. It is hoped that no effort will be spared to avoid the necessity for taking this step and that the new Government in Germany will find it possible to participate fully in the international conferences that are about to be held in Washington and London.

FRANCE

From the economic point of view, the year 1932 has been less satisfactory than any year since the end of the World War. In 1930 and 1931 France was able to resist the effects of the world business depression, but the year 1932 was marked by a conjunction of unfavorable developments— large budgetary deficits, a sharp decline in exports, great falling off in tourist expenditures, lower income from foreign investments, increase in unemployment, continued hoarding of currency, and a deficit in the balance of international payments.

The index number of production, base 1913 = 100, declined from 111 in December, 1931, to 98 in December, 1932. Production of pig iron declined from 8,220,000 tons in 1931 to 5,549,000 tons in 1932; production of crude steel, from 7,812,000 tons to 5,604,000 tons; production of coal, from 51,060 million tons to 47,258,000 tons, and imports of coal from 28,000,000 tons to 20,917,000 tons. The number of unemployed, which averaged 54,588 in 1931, increased to 303,000 in March, 1932. The slight revival of activity in the summer of 1932 resulted in a decrease in unemployment, but at the end of the year the total number of unemployed was 277,000. The situation was not improved in the first part of 1933. On March 4 there were 332,000 workers fully un- employed.

Balance of International Payments

The value of imports in 1932 was $1,169 million as com- pared with $1,654 million in 1931. The corresponding figures for the value of exports are $772 million and $1,193 million. The surplus of commodity imports in 1932 was $397 million, as compared with $461 million, in 1931. The reduction in the surplus of commodity imports is regarded as a favorable development, but it does not indicate an improvement in the French balance of international payments in 1932. The decline in income from tourist expenditures, shipping services, and foreign investments was greater than the decline in the surplus of commodity imports. The French balance of international payments for the years 1929 to 1932 is shown in Table 11.[1]

TABLE 11: BALANCE OF INTERNATIONAL PAYMENTS, FRANCE, 1929 TO 1932[2]

In millions

Item	1929		1930		1931		1932	
	Francs	Dol-lars	Francs	Dol-lars	Francs	Dol-lars	Francs	Dol-lars
Debits								
Surplus of commodity imports..............	10,300	404	13,000	510	13,300	521	10,133	397
Immigrant remittances..	2,500	98	2,500	98	1,800	71	900	35
Total debits.......	12,800	502	15,500	608	15,100	592	11,033	432
Credits								
Net receipts from tourists	8,500	333	8,500	333	6,000	235	4,000	157
Net income from foreign investments.........	5,800	227	5,100	200	4,000	157	3,000	117
Net receipts from reparations..............	4,500	176	4,800	188	1,300	51	..	..
Net receipts from shipping services, insurance, and transit.....	3,600	141	3,100	122	2,700	106	1,800	71
Total credits.......	22,400	878	21,500	843	14,000	549	8,800	345
Surplus (+) or deficit (−) on current account....	+9,600	+376	+6,000	+235	−1,100	−43	−2,233	−87

The most striking change in the balance since 1930 is the enormous loss that France has suffered through the elimination of reparation payments. As a matter of fact, the surpluses in the international transactions of France in the post-war years were to a large extent due to the net income that she had on account of intergovernmental debts and reparations. In 1929 this net income, consisting of receipts

[1] For the years 1929 to 1931, the figures are taken from the annual estimates of Mr. Pierre Meynial. For 1932, the figures of "invisible" items are estimates of the author.

[2] Colonial trade included in 1929, 1930, and 1931.

7

from the reparations minus payments to the United States and Great Britain on account of war debts, amounted to 4,500 million francs. In 1930 the net income from this source was 4,800 million francs. In 1931, owing to the Hoover moratorium, the net amount of reparation receipts was reduced to 1,300 million francs. In 1932 it disappeared altogether under the Lausanne Agreement. The net surplus that France had available before 1930 in her balance of payments for investment abroad and for accumulation of gold was converted into a deficit of 1,100 million francs in 1931. In 1932 this deficit was doubled, according to estimates made in Table 11.

In view of this deficit on account of current international transactions, how was France able to add 14,951 million francs, $586.1 million, to her holdings of gold in 1932? The answer lies partly in the reduction of foreign exchange holdings of the Bank of France and partly in the flow of capital to France. In 1932, the foreign exchange holdings of the Bank of France declined 17,931 million francs, $702.9 million. This decline was 2,980 million francs, $116.8 million, greater than the increase in gold reserves. The reduction in foreign exchange holdings alone was sufficient to account for the import of gold and for the estimated deficit in current international transactions.[1]

In order to obtain a complete picture of the French balance of payments, it would be necessary to have a record of capital movements to and from France. Unfortunately, there is no information on this subject. It is well known that in recent years there has been a considerable flight of foreign funds to France from the countries in which unstable currency or political conditions had frightened investors. The extent of this capital movement, however, is not known. Similarly, there is little or no information in regard to any new foreign loans or repurchase of French foreign issues that may have been made in 1932.

The available information, however, is sufficient to show that in 1932 France had a considerable deficit in her international transactions. Under existing conditions imports of gold cannot take place except through further flow of

[1] Monthly Reports of the Bank of France.

foreign funds to France for safe-keeping or through the sale of long-term foreign securities held by French nationals and their conversion into gold. Neither of these developments is likely to occur on a large scale. Most of the countries of the world, including the United States, have taken measures to prevent the flight of capital, while the financial position of those countries that have not introduced any restrictions on foreign exchange transactions and gold exports is not inferior to that of France.

In the first three months of 1933, gold began to flow out of France. By the end of March the gold reserves of the Bank of France were reduced by about $100 million, as compared with the maximum amount held in November, 1932, while the holdings of foreign exchange declined by about $20 million. Meanwhile, the balance of merchandise trade showed a large increase in the surplus of commodity imports. If there is no improvement in the balance of trade during the remainder of the year, the surplus of imports will exceed 12,000 million francs, $470 million.

Financial and Currency Conditions

The fiscal difficulties of the Government were temporarily solved by the adoption by the Chamber of Deputies at the end of March of the Government's finance bill providing for expenditures of 50,000 million francs, $1,960 million, and revenues of 46,000 million francs, $1,803 million. The larger part of the estimated deficit of about 4,000 million francs, $157 million, can be met by suspending the sinking fund payments, and the Government may not be forced to borrow more than 500 million francs, $20 million, to balance its accounts. The reduction of the budgetary deficits by about 10,000 million francs, $392 million, without the imposition of any new taxes is regarded as a significant accomplishment. The adoption of the budget was accompanied by rather violent political debates in the Chamber, which threatened for a while the existence of the Government. The victory of the Government was due to the breach that occurred in the ranks of the Socialist Party on the question of the military appropriation. A majority of the socialist members supported the Government against the socialist minority, which demanded a reduction of 10% in the military appropriation.

On the whole, the political situation in France is not satisfactory from the point of view of the investing public.[1] The lack of any definite majority in the Chamber of Deputies and the ease with which any government can be overthrown have created a feeling of uncertainty and are no doubt in some measure responsible for the hoarding of money that has been taking place in France in the last two years.

The extent of this currency hoarding is not precisely known. The total amount of Bank of France notes in circulation increased from 67,769 million francs, $2,657 million, at the end of 1929 to 83,546 million francs, $3,275 million, at the end of 1931. During 1932 there was no increase, the amount of notes in circulation at the end of the year being 82,720 million francs, $3,243 million. It is significant, however, that, although the total amount of notes in 1932 showed a decline, the amount of 500 and 1,000 franc notes increased during the year from 52,658 million francs, $2,064 million, to 52,883 million francs, $2,077 million, or 0.4%. From 1930 to 1931, the total amount of notes in circulation increased 9.7%, while there was an increase of 18.0% in the volume of bank notes of large denominations.

As a matter of fact, the entire increase in the amount of currency in circulation during the last two years, or even since 1928, was due to the increase in currency of large denominations. During the last four years, the number of paper notes of 100 francs or less has shown no increase, while the circulation of notes of 500 francs or more increased from 33,720 million francs, $1,322 million, at the end of 1928 to 52,883 million francs, $2,077 million, at the end of 1932.

Most of the commercial transactions in France are carried on with paper money. Notes of large denominations are not suitable as means of payment, and it may be assumed that practically the entire increase in the volume of currency outstanding in denominations of 500 francs or more, amounting to about 20,000 million francs, $784 million, has been due in the last four years to hoarding by French nationals and to some extent by foreigners. The total amount of money

---

[1] It should be observed, however, that the advent of the Hitler régime in Germany has tended to consolidate French public opinion and reduce the danger of extreme political party dissensions.

hoarded at the present time in France, including currency hoarded before 1929 and gold not surrendered to the Bank of France, is estimated at over 35,000 million francs, $1,372 million.[1]

The magnitude of this hoarding and the accumulation of a large volume of foreign funds in France, which may be withdrawn at a moment's notice, have created a grave problem for the financial authorities of France. Undoubtedly the French reserve of gold is more than sufficient to meet any ordinary demands of industry and trade, but the position becomes less satisfactory when the possibilities of foreign capital withdrawals, the movement of funds from France for investment in foreign countries, and the apparently insatiable demand of the French people for currency are taken into consideration.

The course of economic developments in France in 1933 will depend to a large extent on the condition of internal politics and on the success or failure of the International Economic Conference that is to be held in the coming summer. The French are vitally interested in a revival of world trade, although they depend less on it than many other countries, in view of the fine balance between agriculture and manufacturing industries that characterizes the French national economy. France is a great creditor nation and depends on the rest of the world for supplies of some of the most important raw materials. Furthermore, as a great colonial power and as a country with a stationary population, surrounded by nations with increasing populations and strong ambitions for territorial expansion—an expansion that can take place only at the expense of France or of her European allies— France has to rely in a marked degree on international cooperation in the maintenance of world peace.

ITALY

Italy is a country where planned economy is practised on a grand scale, with the object of making Italy independent of foreign countries in regard to food supplies and substan-

[1] Société d'Etudes et d'Informations Economiques, "Bulletin Quotidien," Paris, March 17, 1933, pp. R1-R10.

tially to increase manufacturing production in the face of a great lack of coal and raw materials.

The agricultural program of the Government has so far been attended with considerable success. The output of wheat in 1932 amounted to 7.5 million tons, as compared with an average annual production of 6.6 million tons in the period 1926 to 1931. The production of corn during the same period was increased from 1.8 million tons to 2.8 million tons. The Italian Government is conducting vast reclamation and land amelioration projects, the object of which is not only to expand the agricultural production of Italy, but also to provide unemployment relief during the current business depression.

The main instrument of industrial policy employed by the Government, under strict central control, is deflation in the form of industrial reorganization, reductions of capital, decreases in wages, salaries, and prices. This policy is accompanied by intensive propaganda to stimulate the purchase of home-produced materials and the use of Italian ships in import and export trade and passenger travel.

In the industrial and commercial field, however, the success of the policy of deflation cannot yet be discerned. The average number of unemployed workers in 1932 was 1,006,-442, as compared with 734,454 in the preceding year and 425,437 in 1930. At the end of February, 1933, unemployment was 1,230,000 or about 100,000 higher than a year ago. Building permits[1] in 17 cities, representing the most sensitive index of industrial activity, declined from 92,506 in 1931 to 74,051 in 1932.

The value of exports declined from $523 million in 1931 to $358 million in 1932, or 31.5%. During the same period the value of imports declined from $606 million to $435 million, or 28.2%. There are no reliable estimates of the Italian balance of international payments. It is likely, however, that the favorable items in that balance—income from tourist expenditures, shipping services, and emigrant remittances—although greatly reduced in 1932, was more than sufficient to cover the deficit on account of merchandise trade amounting to $77 million. In view of the favorable

[1] Number of rooms.

balance of international payments, it is difficult to account for the loss of foreign exchange reserves that occurred in 1932 without a corresponding increase in the holdings of gold. In 1932 the foreign exchange reserve of the Bank of Italy declined from 2,170 million lire, $114 million, to 1,304 million lire, $69 million, while the gold reserve increased from 5,626 million lire, $296 million, to 5,839 million lire, $307 million. At the end of March, 1933, the holdings of gold were 6,291 million lire, $331 million, while the foreign exchange reserve amounted to only 802 million lire, $42 million.

The fiscal year ended June 30, 1932, showed a deficit of 4,274 million lire, $225 million. Revenues amounted to 19,033 million lire, $1,001 million, and expenditures to 23,308 million lire, $1,226 million. At the end of February, 1933, the internal debt of the Italian Government was 96,495 million lire, $5,076 million, showing an increase of about 5,000 million lire, $263 million, since the end of 1931. In February, 1933, the budget deficit amounted to 2,653 million lire, $140 million, and was slowly increasing.

Under the Italian form of government the economic activities of the country are subject to governmental direction and control. The Government has devised a comprehensive program of industrial and financial reconstruction that aims, on the one hand, to relieve the commercial banks of a large volume of frozen industrial investments and, on the other, to provide industry and trade with new funds by means of an indirect government guarantee of private obligations.[1] This policy has been successful in preventing bankruptcies of some of the leading financial institutions of Italy, but it has not arrested the depressing effects of deflation.

OTHER EUROPEAN COUNTRIES

Belgium

Belgium is one of the very few countries of the world that has remained consistently faithful to the principles of free international trade. The opponents of excessive tariff protec-

[1] For an analysis of the economic program of the Italian Government see Antonio S. Beni, "Business Reorganization in Italy," Conference Board Information Service: Foreign Affairs, Memorandum No. 6, May 12, 1933.

tion point to Belgium as presenting definite proof that tariffs and other restrictions on foreign trade are futile as measures both of maintaining a higher level of internal business activity and of preventing an adverse balance of merchandise trade. On the whole, the level of industrial and commercial activity in Belgium in 1932 compares favorably with the situation in the leading protectionist countries—Germany, Italy, the United States, Hungary, Jugoslavia, and so on. The value of exports declined from $643 million in 1931 to $412 million in 1932, or 35.9%. During the same period the value of imports declined from $660 million to $452 million, or 31.5%. The import surplus in 1932 was higher than in 1931, but was considerably lower than in 1930 or 1929. The index number of industrial production, base, 1928 = 100 averaged 67.7 in 1932, but the average would have been considerably higher had there been no strike in the coal mines in July and August. In 1932 the metallurgical industry operated at 68% of its record production of 1929. The average number of unemployed workers in 1932 amounted to 161,468, as compared with 79,186 in the preceding year.

The least satisfactory aspect of the Belgian situation is the financial position of the Government. The Government has not been able to balance the budget, and owing to its inability to borrow in the internal market, it was forced to borrow abroad on unusually difficult terms. The fiscal difficulties caused the resignation of the Government in October, 1932. General elections were held in November, but contrary to expectations and to the trend in France, the Socialist Party showed only a slight increase in strength, and the conservative cabinet of Count de Broqueville was able to remain in power. Since that time the Government was able to obtain a short-term loan in Paris, and the Parliament adopted a new finance bill providing for an approximate balance between revenues and expenditures.

The Netherlands

The Netherlands is a great colonial power. Its prosperity is determined in a large measure by its ability to buy and sell freely in the markets of the world. The adoption of tariff protectionism by Great Britain and the outbreak of economic nationalism in Germany are regarded by the Dutch as one of the chief causes of their economic difficulties. For many years the Netherlands has been a free trade country. Recently the Government has introduced a system of import quotas, subsidies, and credits to various branches of agriculture. These measures are considered to be temporary in the hope that the World Economic Conference would result in a general return to more liberal commercial policies. In the meantime the Netherlands has concluded an agreement with Belgium and Luxembourg which provides for a percentage reduction of trade barriers[1] and under which the contracting parties undertake not to increase customs duties and not to introduce new protective duties against each other. This agreement—known as the Convention of Ouchy—violates the spirit of the most-favored-nation clause. It has led to protests on the part of some countries, while others regard it as a dangerous method of tariff disarmament.[2]

The value of exports amounted to $340 million in 1932, as compared with $527 million in the preceding year. The corresponding figures for imports are $522 million and $761 million. Exports show a decline of 35.5% and imports, 31.4%. In spite of the greater percentage decline in exports, the surplus of commodity imports was reduced from $234 million in 1931 to $182 million in 1932. While the Netherlands must have suffered a severe reduction in the income from shipping services and foreign investments, there is no doubt that its balance of international payments was favorable in 1932. Owing to an almost complete cessation of foreign lending in the last two years, the Netherlands has taken its net income in the balance of payments in the form of gold imports. The gold reserve of the Nederlandsche Bank increased from $171 million at the end of 1930 to $415 million at the end of 1932. In the last half of 1932 the Bank's holdings of gold remained practically unchanged, but considerable purchases of gold were made by the large private banks that did not find it profitable to sell gold to the

---

[1] See E. Heldring, "The Convention of Ouchy," Conference Board Information Service: Foreign Affairs, Memorandum No. 7.

[2] See the Annual Address of Mr. R. P. Duchemin, President of the Confédération Générale de la Production Française, delivered at the meeting of the Confederation in Paris on March 24, 1933.

8

Central Bank.[1] The price at which the Central Bank is willing to sell gold is higher than the market price, so that exports and imports of gold are taking place without being reflected in the balance sheet of the Nederlandsche Bank.

A favorable aspect of the situation in the Netherlands is the strong financial position of the Government. Although the budget has not been balanced, the existing deficit is not causing any anxiety to investors. The credit of the Government is very good, as shown by its ability to obtain a long-term loan of 296 million guilders at 5%, issued at par in January, 1933. The cost of short-term loans to the Government is less than 1% per year. This situation is due to the abundance of funds in the market and the impossibility of finding desirable investments in private enterprise.

Sweden

The developments in Sweden received a great deal of attention in 1932 owing to the stability of the wholesale price index and the claims made by the advocates of the so-called stable-money economists that Sweden had accomplished the aim of currency management by stabilizing its price level. In each quarter of 1932 the index number of wholesale prices, base, 1913 = 100, averaged exactly 109. This stability, however, came to an end in the first three months of 1933. The index number declined from 108 in December, 1932, to 106 in January and to 105 in March, 1933. In commenting on the monetary policy of the Central Bank—the Riksbank—one of the largest banking houses in Sweden reaches the following conclusion:

> "If the monetary policy of the Riksbank has thus been accompanied by a rather marked stability in the Swedish krona relatively to the gold currencies, it has not been able to prevent a continuous fall of domestic commodity prices."[2]

Sweden was severely affected by the contraction of production and increase in unemployment in the first half of 1932. In the second half of the year and in the first quarter of 1933, however, the volume of production showed marked

[1] Amsterdamsche Bank, "Financial and Economic Review," January, 1933, p. 21.

[2] Skandinaviska Kreditaktiebolaget, "Quarterly Report," April, 1933, p. 37.

improvement.   The index number of production, base, 1928 = 100, rose from 71.2 in July, 1932, to 83.7 in December and to 85.6 in February, 1933.

The value of exports declined from $283 million in 1931 to $174 million in 1932, or 38.5%.   During the same period the value of imports decreased from $357 million to $212 million, or 40.6%.   The surplus of commodity imports was reduced from $75 million in 1931 to $38 million in 1932.   Sweden is a creditor country.   The reduction in the surplus of imports assures a favorable balance of international payments in 1932.   This accomplishment would not have been possible had Sweden decided to adhere to the gold standard.   The holdings of gold remained unchanged in 1932 at $55 million.

After a period of money stringency, following the abandonment of the gold standard and the Kreuger crash, money rates began to decline and the money market was characterized by an abundance of liquid funds in the commerical banks.   The discount rate of the Riksbank was reduced from 6% to 5% in February, 1932, and to 3.5% in September, 1932, at which point it remains at the present time.[1]

Sweden is one of the very few countries in the world that has balanced its national budget.   During the first half of the fiscal year ending June 30, 1933, revenues amounted to 337.8 million kronor and expenditures to 392.7 million kronor.   The apparent deficit in the first half of the year was due to the change in regulations in regard to the payment of income and property taxes.[2]   The 1933–34 budget has been balanced at a total of 1,029 million kronor.

The Succession States

The states among whom the territory of Austria-Hungary[3] was partitioned after the World War—Czechoslovakia, Austria, Hungary, Rumania, and Jugoslavia—have been violently affected by the business depression.   Czechoslovakia is the only exception to this statement owing to a fine balance between its agriculture and industry and the ab-

---

[1] May, 1933.

[2] Swedish Board of Trade, "The Swedish Economic Review," March, 1933, p. 4.

[3] Italy and Poland belong to this group of states, but as a rule they are not included among the Succession States.

sence of internal political difficulties. In 1932 Czechoslovakia had the honor of being the only succession state which met all its foreign obligations, whose currency was quoted on the foreign exchange markets of the world, and one of the very small number of countries that were able to secure a loan[1] in the French money market.

The situation in the other Succession States may be described as bordering on bankruptcy. In some states this bankruptcy is not only economic but also political. For centuries before the World War this part of Europe was a center of political instability and international disturbance. This state of affairs has not been materially improved by the destruction of the "political monster" ruled over by the Hapsburg dynasty and by the practical expulsion of the Turks from the Balkan Peninsula. The penetration of Albania by Italy, the territorial demands of Hungary, the Macedonian aspirations of Bulgaria, the Rumanian fear of Russia, and the Austrian demand for a customs union with Germany make this part of the world an ideal place for the practice of what is known as pre-war diplomacy—military alliances, intrigues, and so on. The importance of genuine political disarmament, as a step to economic disarmament, is strikingly demonstrated in the Danube basin. International political disarmament, however, must be preceded by internal political consolidation of the countries in this area. Open and concealed dictatorships that do not rest on any class or section of the people but are imposed on the people by a small group of persons in high office who control the military organization, represent a danger to international peace. In countries, where all discussion of domestic difficulties is prohibited through strict censorship of the press, criticism of foreign countries is allowed and foreign policies are used to divert the attention of the people from internal political troubles.

From the economic and political point of view the situation in Austria is more favorable than that in the South Eastern states of Europe. This is due partly to a better internal political situation and partly to the assistance that Austria has received from the League of Nations. The national budget of Austria is practically balanced. The schil-

[1] 600 million francs.

ling rate of exchange was stable throughout 1932, but quotations were purely nominal. The value of exports declined from $184 million in 1931 to $106 million in 1932, or 42.4%. During the same period imports declined from $304 million to $194 million, or 36.2%, and the surplus of commodity imports was reduced from $120 million to $88 million.

The business depression in Hungary, Jugoslavia, and Rumania has created a situation of almost complete national insolvency. These countries depend on agricultural exports, and the extraordinary decline in the prices of farm products, combined with the protective measures adopted by the industrial countries of Europe, has forced them to default on their foreign debts and to adopt special laws to lighten the burden of internal indebtedness on the farmer. The budgetary situation is very unsatisfactory, with falling revenues, heavy taxation, and growing deficits.

Poland

Of the agricultural countries of Europe, Poland has shown the best record of economic and financial stability and political tranquillity. The domestic political situation, however, cannot be regarded as normal owing to the presence of underground forces that are anxious to break the political system established by Marshal Pilsudski. In the field of foreign relations Poland has been able to improve its position through the conclusion of a Non-Aggression Treaty with Soviet Russia, but this improvement was somewhat offset by the threatening situation created on the Western frontier of Poland through the establishment of an extremely nationalistic government in Germany. The international position of Poland is not enviable. Faced with Germany on the west, that demands the removal of the Polish Corridor, and with Soviet Russia on the east that can scarcely be regarded as a friend, Poland must rely for her security on defensive alliances with the countries composing the French bloc in European politics.

The satisfactory achievements in the economic field in 1932 were the payment of interest on foreign debts,[1] a large

[1] With the exception of the December payment to the United States on account of intergovernmental debts.

excess of exports over imports, and the maintenance of a stable exchange without the imposition of rigid restrictions on exchange transactions. The increase in the surplus of commodity exports, however, was accompanied by an enormous decline in the value of foreign trade. The value of exports declined from $211 million in 1931 to $122 million in 1932, or 42.2%. The value of imports decreased from $164 million to $97 million, or 40.9%. In 1932 the value of exports was 61.4% lower than in 1929. During the same period the decline in the value of imports amounted to 72.2%.

The unsatisfactory aspects of the situation are an unbalanced budget, a marked decline in industrial activity, and a ruinous fall in agricultural prices that has necessitated a virtual suspension of debt payments by the farmers. The Government is practicing a policy of deflation in an attempt to adjust the burden of indebtedness to the reduced profit of business and agriculture.[1] A number of laws and decrees have been issued for the purpose of reducing the rate of interest on existing debts and extending the term of repayment.[2] Among the important financial reforms in 1932 was the abandonment of the gold-exchange standard in favor of the gold-bar standard.

CANADA

As in all other agricultural countries, the situation in Canada in 1932 was dominated by the disastrous decline in prices of agricultural commodities. Contrary to the trend in many other countries, wholesale prices declined throughout the year and in the first two months of 1933. The index number of industrial production, prepared by the Dominion Bureau of Statistics, also declined steadily. The exchange rate of the Canadian dollar remained relatively stable during the year, fluctuating between 91% and 86% of its par value. The decline in construction activity was particularly great. The value of new construction was lower than in any other year since 1918. The budget of the Dominion Government

[1] Bank Gospodarstwa Krajovego, "Monthly Review," December, 1932, pp. 1-3.
[2] The Bank of Poland, Bulletin No. 9 of the Economic Research Department, Warsaw, 1933, pp. 151-152.

has not been balanced, and the deficit is considerably increased by the necessity of meeting the deficit of the Canadian National Railways, amounting to about $50 million, and by the growing cost of unemployment relief.

The value of Canadian exports declined from $595 million in 1931 to $435 million in 1932, or 26.9%. During the same period the value of imports declined from $611 million to $399 million, or 34.7%. For the first time since 1928 Canada had a surplus of commodity exports in 1932. This achievement, however, was accompanied by a tremendous decline in the total value of trade. The combined value of exports and imports in 1932 was $374 million lower than the value of exports alone in 1929. Owing to the creation of a surplus of commodity exports Canada's balance of international payments was more favorable in 1932 than in the preceding year. Canada is a debtor country in the sense that her interest payments to foreign holders of Canadian securities are greater than her income from Canadian investments in foreign countries. Canada, however, has a large income from tourist expenditures. In normal years, this income is sufficient to provide the necessary funds for the service on the foreign debt. According to preliminary estimates of the balance of payments, published in the "Financial Post" of Toronto, the net income from tourist expenditures in 1932 amounted to $127 million, and the net payment to foreign countries on account of their investments in Canada was $160 million.[1] The value of gold exports in 1932 was $63 million.

Favorable aspects of the Canadian situation were the strength of the banking system and the absence of political difficulties or social unrest. Canada is in a good position to benefit immediately from a revival of activity. In the spring of 1933 there were visible signs of economic recovery, owing to increasing prices of agricultural commodities and raw materials. There were also certain indications that the Canadian Government would abandon the policy of deflation and enter into an agreement with the other leading powers of the world to raise world prices.

[1] Figures in Canadian currency, "The Economist," April 1, 1933, p. 685.

SOUTH AMERICAN COUNTRIES

The economic situation in the South American countries in 1932 was one of extreme difficulty. From 1924 to 1929 the economic development in these countries was greatly promoted by the large inflow of foreign long-term funds. The cessation of foreign lending and the disastrous decline in prices of agricultural commodities and raw materials in the last three years have practically destroyed the purchasing power of these countries and exerted a tremendous strain on their balance of international payments. In order to protect their exchanges, these countries were forced to adopt severe restrictions on foreign exchange transactions and to suspend interest and amortization payments on their foreign debts. In addition, they have introduced prohibitive import duties and complete upward revisions of their tariffs in an attempt to maintain a favorable balance of merchandise trade.

The effect of these measures has actually been to create a surplus of commodity exports, but at the cost of an almost total destruction of foreign trade. Revival of international trade in this part of the world requires, in the first place, a marked increase in agricultural and raw material prices and, in the second place, an adjustment of the foreign indebtedness. The creditor countries will no doubt be called upon to make sacrifices through the reduction of interest payments on the outstanding debts. It may be expected also that with a revival in activity, stimulated by increasing prices, it will be safe and profitable to extend new loans to some of the leading and economically powerful South American states.

Argentina

Business activity reached a new low level in 1932. The principal factor in this downward movement was the decline in meat prices, which is one of the principal exports of Argentina. The value of exports declined from $428 million in 1931 to $331 million in 1932, or 22.7%, while imports declined from $345 million to $215 million, or 37.7%. From 1929 to 1932 the decline in exports was 63.5%, and that of imports, 73.8%.

The Government has not been able to balance the budget,

but the deficit will be very small, amounting only to about 30 million pesos. The budget for 1933 provides for revenues of 827 million pesos, $213 million, and expenditures of 821 million pesos, $212 million. The national floating debt was reduced during the year from 1,267 million pesos, $327 million, to 885 million pesos, $228 million. The reduction was accomplished by issuing long-term bonds. The total national funded debt on June 13, 1932, amounted to 2,730 million pesos, $704 million. Of this amount the external debt represented 967 million pesos, $249 million. The Government of Argentina was able in 1932 to meet punctually the service on the internal and external funded debt. This, however, was not true of the Argentine provinces and municipalities which have been forced to suspend payments on their foreign obligations.

In April, 1933, Sir Otto Niemayer, who came to Argentina in January, 1933, at the invitation of the Argentine Government to study the economic situation, issued a series of recommendations designed to rehabilitate the financial system of Argentina. Sir Otto suggested that the present Conversion Office, Exchange Control Commission, and the Rediscount Commission be abolished and a Central Bank created to take over their functions.[1] Sir Otto also recommended abolition of the existing dual systems of gold and paper currency within a year after the establishment of a Central Bank, and urged a thoroughgoing reform of the cumbersome system of official accounting. In regard to the immediate future, removal of exchange restrictions was not advised owing to the impossibility of creating a sufficiently large surplus of exports to permit free dealings in foreign exchange. Throughout 1932 and the first quarter of 1933 the Argentine peso was officially pegged at 59 cents or 60% of its par value.

Brazil

The economic difficulties of Brazil were caused largely by the ruinous decline in the price of coffee. The situation was

[1] Mr. Carlos A. Tornquist, "The Gold Movement and Argentine Monetary Policy," National Industrial Conference Board, "A Picture of World Economic Conditions in the Summer of 1929," New York, 1929, pp. 291–297.

9

further aggravated by the revolution in the state of Sao Paulo that lasted from July until October, 1932. During the revolution there was a complete cessation of coffee exports from that state, producing a state of demoralization in the coffee markets. The present Federal Government appears to be firmly established. On February 1, 1933, the military government in Sao Paulo was replaced by a civil government, ending the state of siege. General elections for President and Congress were held throughout Brazil on May 3, 1933.

Since the quelling of the revolution in October, 1932, the Federal Government has taken energetic measures to improve the economic and financial situation. The principal economic problem of Brazil is to increase the price of coffee. The ineffectiveness of past policies, attempting to maintain a high price without any reduction of output, has been clearly demonstrated, and in November, 1932, the Government issued a decree prohibiting the planting of coffee for a period of three years. In the meantime, the destruction of surplus coffee stocks of inferior grades is continuing. Up to January 31, 1933, a total of 13,578,000 bags of coffee has been destroyed. Especially helpful to the coffee industry was the reduction in the heavy export taxes on coffee, in December, 1932.

The exchange value of the milreis was maintained at a nominal rate of about 7.62 cents, or 36% below par, in the second half of 1932 and the first quarter of 1933. In the actual market, however, the exchange could be bought for as low as four cents per milreis. Brazil has no gold reserves, and the exchange is controlled by the Bank of Brazil. The system of foreign exchange control practised by the Bank is extremely rigid, with the result that imports have practically come to a standstill. The value of imports declined from $417 million in 1929 to $105 million in 1932, or 74.8%. During the same period, the value of exports was reduced from $456 million to $182 million, or 60.1%. Revival of foreign trade and general economic activity cannot take place without a substantial increase in the price of coffee.

THE FAR EASTERN COUNTRIES

The situation in the Far East was dominated throughout the year 1932 by the conflict between China and Japan over the possession of Manchuria. Through the action taken by the League of Nations against Japan and through the refusal of the countries of the world to recognize the state of Manchukuo as an independent and sovereign country, the Sino-Japanese dispute has assumed international importance.[1] It was followed by Japan's resignation from the League of Nations and has raised the delicate question of whether or not that resignation implies that the Pacific Islands, given to Japan under the mandate of the League, will have to be surrendered by Japan and their administration entrusted to some other country. The Japanese Government has announced in no misleading terms that its withdrawal from the League of Nations in no way affected its right to the possession of mandated territories. It is impossible to foresee at the present time in what manner this dispute will be settled. There is no doubt that the situation is grave and that it involves not only the countries belonging to the League of Nations, but also the United States and Soviet Russia.

Japan

The economic developments in Japan in 1932 were determined largely by the military needs of the Government and the depreciation of the yen. During 1932 the exchange value of the yen declined from 36 cents to 21 cents, that is, from 72% to 42% of its gold parity. Currency depreciation was accompanied by rising commodity prices. The index number of wholesale prices, base, 1913 = 100, increased from 120.5 in January, 1932, to 139.8 a year later. In the first quarter of 1933 exchange depreciation was stopped, putting an end to speculative activities, reversing the trend of commodity prices, and bringing about a general decline in business activity. The iron and steel construction industries, however, did not follow the downward movement,

---

[1] See Mr. Li Ming and Mr. S. Ikeda, "Economic Aspects of Sino-Japanese Relations," Conference Board Information Service: Foreign Affairs, Memorandum No. 3, March 31, 1933.

owing to the demand of the Government for military materials and the construction of public works.[1] The depreciation in the American dollar in April, 1933, was received with little favor in Japan, its effect being to increase the exchange value of the yen and to exert a deflationary effect on prices.

In terms of the Japanese yen, the foreign trade of Japan showed a marked increase in 1932, but, in terms of gold, imports declined 36.1% and exports, 32.3%. The value of exports declined from $566 million in 1931 to $383 million in 1932. During the same period the value of imports declined from $610 million to $390 million. The surplus of commodity imports was greater in 1931 than in 1932, but the balance of international payments was no doubt favorable. An estimate of the balance of international payments in 1932 is shown in Table 12.[2]

TABLE 12: BALANCE OF INTERNATIONAL PAYMENTS, JAPAN, 1932

In millions

Item	Yen	Dollars
Credits		
Commodity exports	1,410.0	396.4
Income from foreign investments	150.0	42.2
Emigrant remittances	104.0	29.2
Shipping services	150.0	42.2
Insurance	1.0	0.3
Tourist expenditures	35.0	9.8
Total	1,850.0	520.0
Debits		
Commodity imports	1,431.0	402.3
Foreign debt services	215.0	60.4
Expenditures of Japanese tourists abroad	55.5	15.6
Immigrant remittances	17.0	4.8
Government expenditures abroad	20.0	5.6
Total	1,738.5	488.7

The financial position of the Government is regarded with considerable concern, in view of the enormous increase in

[1] Mitsubishi Economic Research Bureau, "Monthly Circular," Tokyo, March, 1933, pp. 1–3.

[2] Estimated by Mr. Kenji Kodama, President of the Yokohama Specie Bank. See Société d'Etudes et d'Informations Economiques, "Japon," Paris, March, 1933, p. 23.

expenditures and in the public debt. The budget for the current fiscal year is the largest in the history of Japan. The total expenditures are estimated at 2,238 million yen, $472 million. Of this amount, extraordinary expenditures account for 881 million yen, $186 million. These expenditures are to be met entirely by borrowing. Military expenditures alone are estimated at 821 million yen, $173 million. This enormous program of government financing may easily lead to currency inflation, which has so far been avoided. The note circulation of the Bank of Japan in February, 1933, was 1,066 million yen, $222 million, or about the same as a year ago. A month later, however, the note circulation showed an increase of almost 200 million yen, $45 million. The gold reserve remained practically unchanged during the year at slightly over $200 million, owing to the prohibition of gold exports.

The development of economic affairs in Japan in 1933 will depend to a large extent on the monetary policy of the Government. If resort is taken to currency inflation as a means of satisfying the borrowing demands of the Government, prices will undoubtedly rise and business activity maintained at the high level reached in 1932. This process, however, cannot continue indefinitely, and Japan will be faced with the necessity of stabilizing its currency and balancing its budget. Obviously, the situation in Japan will be greatly influenced by the outcome of the forthcoming World Economic Conference. A general increase in world prices and a revival of demand for Japanese exports, especially on the part of the United States, would ease the shock which currency and price stabilization will inevitably produce in Japan.

China

Throughout 1932 economic activity in China was maintained at a high level owing to the steady depreciation of its currency caused by the decline in the price of silver. China is the only important country in the world that uses silver as the standard of value and the basis of its currency. The effect of declining silver prices, therefore, was the same as that of currency depreciation. The effect of higher silver prices would be deflationary if they were not accompanied by counteracting monetary measures.

The value of foreign trade in terms of gold suffered a severe decline during the business depression. In the case of China, currency depreciation did not have its usual effect of stimulating exports and impeding imports. From 1929 to 1932 the value of exports declined 74.5%, while that of imports was reduced only 56.5%. From 1931 to 1932 exports declined 46.5% and imports, 27.4%. This development is partly due to the loss of Manchurian trade. For many years China had had a large surplus of commodity imports, while Manchuria, on the other hand, has regularly exported appreciably more than she imported. If Manchuria is permanently separated from China, the effect on the Chinese balance of international payments will be very unfavorable. The enormous decline in exports was due also to the sharp curtailment in foreign demand for Chinese principal exports —raw silk, peanuts, wood oil, beans, bean oil, and so on. Most of the exports of China are not necessities and, therefore, the demand for them can be drastically reduced in a period of business depression.

In his report for the last two fiscal years, ended June 30, 1932, the Minister of Finance pointed out that[1] "since February, 1932, for the first time in the twenty-one years of the Republic, the Government has been able to balance its budget at a time of world economic depression when practically every government has large deficits and when, in addition to the depression, the Government has had to confront the colossal burden of the 1931 floods, the slump in silver, the Japanese seizure of revenue in Manchuria and the attack on Shanghai."[2] The ability of China to balance its national accounts without recourse to borrowing was reflected in a striking recovery in the price of Chinese bonds in the London market. The quotation of 1913 Reorganization Loan, bearing an interest rate of 5%, increased from the low point of 55 reached in 1932 to 77 on April 5, 1933.[3]

[1] Bureau of Foreign Trade, "Chinese Economic Journal," Shanghai, February, 1933, pp. 210–230.

[2] Ibid., p. 210.

[3] "The Economist," April 8, 1933, p. 762.

Internal political conditions in 1932 were more stable than in previous years.   There was no insurrection against the Central Government, and factional hostilities were relatively unimportant.   The national unity of China, however, cannot be regarded as an accomplished fact.   The task of unifying a continent with 400 million inhabitants, speaking a large number of dialects, cannot be accomplished in a few years.   Improved communication and transportation facilities will be required to establish more intimate contacts among the various provinces and to make it possible for the Central Government to exercise its authority more efficiently in the distant and at present barely accessible parts of the country.

TABLE OF CURRENCY CONVERSION

Foreign currencies were converted into dollars at the following rates of exchange:

Argentina, average per gold peso for 1931, 66.7 cents; for 1932, 58.4 cents.

Australia, average per pound for 1931, 351.5 cents; for 1932, 279.9 cents.

Belgium, par, 2.78 cents per franc.

Brazil, average per paper milreis for 1931, 7.03 cents; for 1932, 7.12 cents.

Canada, average per dollar for 1931, 96.3 cents; for 1932, 88.09 cents.

Chile, average per gold peso for 1931, 12.07 cents; for 1932, 7.9 cents.

Colombia, average per gold peso for 1931, 96.25 cents; for 1932, 95.28 cents.

France, par, 3.92 cents per franc.

Germany, par, 23.82 cents per reichsmark.

Great Britain, average per pound sterling for 1931, 453.50 cents; for 1932, 350.61 cents.

Italy, par, 5.26 cents per lira.

Japan, average per yen for 1931, 48.85 cents; for 1932, 28.11 cents.

Netherlands, par, 40.20 cents per florin.

Sweden, average per krona for 1931, 25.25 cents; for 1932, 18.47 cents.